THEN AND THERE SERIES

GENERAL EDITOR

MARJORIE REEVES, M.A., PH.D.

The Romans in Scotland

OLIVER THOMSON M.A.

Illustrated from contemporary sources

LONGMAN

LONGMAN GROUP LIMITED
London
*Associated companies, branches and representatives
throughout the world*

© Longman Group Ltd 1968

First published 1968
Fifth impression 1974

ISBN 0 582 20416 X

ACKNOWLEDGEMENTS

We are grateful to the following for permission to reproduce the
illustrations in this book:- The British Museum—pages 12, 79, 80 and
85; J. Allan Cash—page 26; Colchester and Essex Museum—page 6;
L. Gliori—pages 46 and 53; Hunterian Museum, photographs by
Douglas Scott—pages 18, 25, 43, 44, 45, 49, 59, 60, 61, 64, 65, 69, 72, 73,
74, 75 and 77; Kilmarnock Museum, photograph by J. Stewart
McLauchlan—page 40; Mansell Collection—pages vi, 31, 32 and 84;
Ministry of Public Buildings and Works—page iv; Ministry of Public
Buildings and Works, Edinburgh—pages 36 and 37; Museo del Vaticano
—page 12 (top); National Museum of Antiquaries, Scotland—pages 41,
70 and 76; National Museum of Wales—page 24; Oxford University
Press—page 66 and J. K. St. Joseph, Cambridge University—page 9.

Thanks are due to Dr. A. Robertson of the Hunterian Museum,
Glasgow, for reading the manuscript.

Printed in Hong Kong by
Commonwealth Printing Press Ltd

CONTENTS

TO THE READER

Have you ever thought what it would be like to have a great frontier like the Iron Curtain running through your back garden? You would probably think it a most odd place to have a frontier, yet the line of one of the most important frontiers in the world once lay right across the central belt of Scotland. This frontier was heavily fortified and constantly patrolled— just as difficult to cross as the Iron Curtain is today—for it separated the great Roman Empire from the savage peoples who lived outside it. The British part of this frontier once lay between the Firths of Forth and Clyde, where traces of it can still be found—perhaps in your back garden.

It is the purpose of this book to explain how the Roman frontier came to lie across the middle of Scotland, what it looked like and where you can still see it. We will also look at the everyday life of the Romans in Scotland and try from their

Hadrian's Wall in Northumberland, first of the two great frontier walls built by the Romans in Britain.

stories to learn something of the great empire from which they came. Many of the things we talk about will have been brought to light quite recently by the work of *archaeologists* , so we will learn a little about the special techniques by which these men have rediscovered vanished Roman forts in Scotland and have pieced together their histories from a number of small clues.

Before we go any further there is one matter which must be cleared up. In the years we are talking about (A.D. 80 to A.D. 410) the Scots, who originally came from Ireland, had not yet settled in our country, so instead of calling it Scotland, which would be incorrect, we will refer to it as North Britain. In the same way the Angles or English had not yet arrived in England so we will call that part of the country South Britain.

Now we can go on and look at ancient North Britain through the eyes of four men who had a great effect on it in Roman times. The first of these is Agricola.

You will find the meaning of words printed like this in the glossary on pages 96-98.

Roman General (not Agricola) addressing his troops—note the standards in the centre

1   Agricola: The First Invasion

We meet Agricola for the first time in the year A.D. 80, when he stands on the banks of the River Tweed with his army and looks northwards at the thickly wooded hills of an unknown country. This man is a Roman general, governor of the *province* of Britain, and he is preparing for the first Roman invasion of the northern part of the island.

We want to find out how and why he came to be here, so let us first of all take a closer look at the man himself as he stands there in his short military tunic, surrounded by the high-ranking officers of his army.

He is not a man of outstanding appearance, yet his weather-beaten features are full of determination and vigour. Below him, listening to his words, you can see the *standard* bearers of his *legions*, wearing their strange lion-skin head-dresses and holding the beautifully *gilded* standards of the army. To lose these in battle would mean perpetual disgrace for the legion. Behind them stand the legionaries with their plumed helmets, armour-plated jerkins and shields. These are the finest soldiers in the Roman army and behind them again stand a few of the cavalrymen who are new recruits from the German province of the Empire. We shall be seeing more of all these men later on, but for the moment let us imagine that we can join them for a while and listen to what Agricola is saying.

'Soldiers, you have campaigned with me now for two years already, one spent defeating the tribes near Mona (Anglesey in Wales), the other bringing the Roman peace to these northern parts of Britain. Now only one threat to the safety of our province remains—these savage barbarians who live in the hills you see ahead. We have already sent scouts ahead into this area and now we are all going north to teach these tribes a lesson, that they cannot invade the province of the Roman emperor with *impunity*. The going will be difficult and we shall have to build roads as we go along, for there are none there at present. I have here a message from the Emperor Vespasian* himself wishing us success and I know that you will give me the same brave and loyal service that I have known since I first came to Britain. Now let us make our sacrifices to the Gods for a victorious campaign.'

The men cheer Agricola when he has finished speaking, for he is a popular and fair-minded general. Certainly he is a tough campaigner and when he first came to Britain as governor surprised everyone by actually starting a war against the tribes of Mona in the autumn, when most people thought the season for fighting was over. But Agricola was keen to show them all that he was no fair-weather general, and his decisive victory in Wales made him the most respected man in Britain. Now he stands aside as the priests come forward to make their sacrifices, a bull, a sheep and a pig for the success of their campaign.

When the ceremony is over Agricola receives some messages from the south, for he has other duties besides the army. He is also extremely concerned about the welfare of the Britons in the new towns which are growing up under Roman rule. They have been somewhat oppressed by previous governors, but now they no longer have to pay extra taxes, but are being encouraged to build up a more civilised existence than they have ever known before. Under Agricola's rule the southern Britons are so content, so prosperous, and so full of respect for Rome that they actually begin to copy Roman dress of their own accord. The *toga* is now a familiar sight in the towns of South Britain.

Let us look once more at this man who has helped so much

---

* For this and other proper names see List on page 90.

to turn the new province of Britain into a civilised part of the Roman Empire. What sort of a man is he and where does he come from? His first names are Gnaeus Julius, good Roman names, and his surname means a 'Farmer' in Latin, the language which the Romans spoke. But, in spite of his names, Agricola was not in fact born in the city of Rome, nor even in Italy. He comes from a small town in the south of France and he went to school in the great city of Massilia (Marseilles) which is one of the largest ports on the Mediterranean. Now this area is part of the Roman province of Gaul, but it has belonged to Rome for so long that many of its people have been made citizens of Rome, so that they can serve in her legions and rise to the highest posts in the government. A man born in Gaul can be a Roman, just as Saint Paul, who was born in Tarsus in Asia Minor, was also a citizen of Rome and was sent to Rome for trial, as you can read in the New Testament. So Agricola, though he has no Italian blood in his veins, is able to become a general in the Roman Army.

Roman in toga

Now we begin to see how a schoolboy from Marseilles could become the Roman governor of Britain, but let us try to find out a little more about his life. He was born in the year A.D. 40,* just a few years after the crucifixion of Christ in

* See date chart on page 89.

Jerusalem, and just three years before the Emperor Claudius first sent his armies to Britain. Agricola's father died soon after he was born, having offended the new emperor and fallen into disgrace. In spite of this, however, when he came of age Agricola was still allowed to wear the special broad purple stripe on his toga which showed people that his father had belonged to the top rank of Roman citizens, the *Senate*. This meant that he too could become an officer with the hope of reaching an important position, and so he was sent to join the army.

So Agricola, who had just lost his mother, killed in her home by some marauding pirates, went off to join Legion XX which was stationed in Britain. Once there he did not have long to wait before he saw his first fighting, because that very year the Iceni, a tribe in Eastern Britain, rebelled and attacked the Roman garrisons. Led by their famous and fierce Queen Boudicca in her chariot, these tribesmen must have made a frightening sight for a fresh young officer, but so far as we know he must have done well, for not long afterwards he was promoted to join the governor's personal staff.

After this Agricola's career went from strength to strength. He saw service in Asia Minor, then spent an awkward year as a city magistrate in Rome during the reign of Nero. Then it was back to Britain again, this time as *legate* or commander of his old legion—XX. We know little of what happened then, but the next year saw Agricola another step up the ladder as governor of a province in Gaul, not so far from his own home town. Now his success was rewarded by the greatest honour of all, when he was made a *consul* in Rome, the highest rank in the Empire under the Emperor himself. Now at the very peak of his career and not yet forty years old, Agricola was to be sent on the most important task of his life, to bring lasting peace to the troubled province of Britain.

Let us rejoin him there on the banks of the Tweed, standing

at the head of his men as they prepare to move northwards. We have seen that in the first months of his governorship he impressed everyone by his quick and efficient suppression of the tribes of Mona. He also made many friends by his honesty and his refusal to accept bribes. As we have seen, the Britons in the south have begun to look on Roman rule as a blessing instead of a burden. They are acquiring new towns, baths,

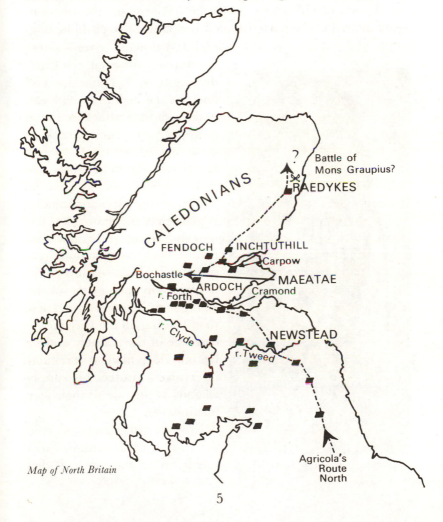

Map of North Britain

5

roads and other benefits from the Romans' skill as engineers. In the north it is a different story. This is still a rough frontier area where the tribes seize any chance to invade and rob the wealthier southerners. Agricola, who has made Wales peaceful in a few months will spend over six years in North Britain and we shall see that he will meet many difficulties there.

First of all he has no proper maps of the country ahead, only the reports of the scouts whom he has sent up the previous year. They have reported that it is a land of steep hills, bogs and fast-flowing rivers where the native tribesmen, the Caledonii and the Maeatae are wild and savage fighters, who can make a sudden attack and then disappear in their trackless wilderness before you have time to recover. With enemies like these Agricola knows that he will have no easy victory and he is glad that his main base has now moved up to the new fortress of York, so that reinforcements will not have quite so far to come in the event of an emergency. There is a good new road leading all the way up the east side of the country and he has built forts along it at regular intervals to protect his supply wagons as they wend their way northwards.

Now the order has been given and the army has moved forwards on to the new wooden

Roman centurien of the Legion XX

bridge over the Tweed, so let us watch as they go past. First come the standard bearers of **XX** Legion with their bodyguards, then the legate of the legion in his horse-drawn chariot, then, one behind the other, the three *cohorts* of this legion which have been chosen to come north. The remaining seven cohorts in the legion have stayed behind to man the forts on the way to York. Now, as we watch the three cohorts marching past, singing their marching songs, we see that each of them is divided into six groups called *centuries*, which consist of eighty men, not a hundred as you might think. In front of each century marches a *centurion*, a hardy, experienced soldier who shouts orders at his men and points angrily at one slowcoach with his special stick made from the wood of a vine. If you count up the number of centuries and cohorts, you should be able to work out how many men there are in one complete legion.

The legionaries who follow are tough well-trained men as well. Each carries two *javelins* or spears, as his main weapon and a largish leather shield, while at his waist hang a short sword on one side and a dagger on the other. He is dressed in a short tunic and a leather jacket with strips of metal sewn on to it to protect his shoulders and chest.

Roman legionary

7

Rolled up and strapped to his back is a long brown cloak which will keep him warm in cold weather and can be used as a blanket to sleep in at night. Apart from this he carries a few personal belongings, his daily ration of oatmeal and a change of clothing. The plume from his helmet has also been tucked away, as it is only required on ceremonial occasions.

Now we see the men of the other two legions go past; IX from York and II from South Wales. Together with XX these legions (not the men!) all formed part of the original army used for the conquest of Britain in A.D. 43, and most of these men have already seen service in many different parts of the island.

So the legions march on and we can note that Agricola has over ten thousand men at his command, for in addition to the nine cohorts of legionaries he has at least the same number again in *auxiliary troops*; mostly they are light infantry and some cavalry recruited from the conquered tribes near the mouth of the Rhine. It is one of the clever tricks by which the Romans keep their old enemies out of mischief and increase the size of their army at the same time—just make soldiers of them and send them to a part of the empire far away from their homes.

Behind the soldiers come the heavy wagons carrying supplies: timber for building forts, tools for digging *ramparts*, cooking utensils, huge jars of wine and oil, *catapults*, wagon wheels, spare weapons, boxes of nails—everything that a Roman army might require.

Meanwhile we follow the front part of the army as it plods on over the hills and it is soon clear that they are not going to meet many enemies. As the Roman army appears, the tribesmen take to the woods, and though there is the odd report of a hairy head peeping over the heather, the sight of this huge force is too much for tribes who have only been used to fighting in quite small groups, and have never been friendly enough with each other to think of uniting now against the common enemy.

As there is no fighting for the time being, let us pause to think for a moment how we know so much that went on at this time. Our knowledge in fact comes from two main sources. One is the work of archaeologists who have excavated the forts which Agricola built along his route. In some cases they have only discovered the fort by aerial photography which shows a slight shading in grass or crops growing over old walls or ditches which are beneath the surface of the ground and invisible to an ordinary observer. Having discovered the fort by this means, the archaeologist can then remove the surface soil and find out what is underneath. Then comes the real detective work of finding small coins, bits of pottery or other clues that will tell the expert when the fort was built. We shall

Aerial photograph of the Roman fort at Birrens, Dumfriesshire. Note rows of ditches and gate on right side of fort

be seeing some more of this work later on but for the moment let us turn to our other great source of information. This is a book which was written about the life of Agricola a few years later by his own son-in-law, a Roman historian called Tacitus. This is one of the few books of the time which have survived, for remember this was many hundreds of years before the invention of printing, and it is the earliest book which tells us anything about the history of North Britain. So far as we know, the author never saw the country for himself, but at least he heard the story of its invasion at first hand from Agricola. Here is his description of the army's first year in North Britain.

'Our army was seriously *buffeted* by storms, but the enemy were too terrified to *molest* it. There was even time to spare for the establishment of forts. It was observed by experts that no general had ever shown a better eye for ground than Agricola. No fort of his was ever stormed, ever surrendered or ever abandoned. They were protected against long sieges by supplies renewed every year. And so winter in these forts had no terrors.'

Agricola in fact built a line of forts between the Firths of Forth and Clyde and we shall have a closer look at what these forts were like shortly. We can get a better idea of them from the ones he built further north which have survived in better shape. Meanwhile Tacitus tells us that:

'The narrow neck of land between the Clyde and Forth was now secured by garrisons and the whole sweep of country to the south was safe in our hands. The enemy had been pushed into what was virtually another island.'

So far Agricola's invasion of North Britain has been a great success.

2   By Land and Sea

When autumn came Agricola returned to his winter quarters in York and while thinking over the events of the past year he seems to have been struck by the importance of using the sea to help conquer the rough hills of North Britain. His ships might be able to navigate the firths and rivers more easily than his armies could march across the moors and bogs. So next spring he sent a small fleet up the coast to *reconnoitre,* and it was some of Agricola's ships which were probably the first to sail round the north of Scotland and prove that Britain was an island. Anyway from now on ships were very important to Agricola, so let us look at what kind of ships the Romans used.

On the next page is a picture of a Roman warship. You will see that she has a sharp ramming device just on the waterline with which she can pierce the hulls of enemy ships and sink them. Her only other methods of fighting are to break the oars of other ships by sailing into them and pulling her own oars in quickly just before hitting the ship, or to run alongside and let the soldiers she carries fight it out with those of the enemy. You can see that the Roman warship is long, thin and fast. She has both a square sail and rows of well-trained oarsmen who are probably slaves or prisoners. These will make her skim over the calm waters of the Mediterranean, but she is not so good in the stormier waters of the North Sea. In fact Agricola may have preferred to use merchant ships for his *reconnoitring*. As you see from the bottom picture on the next page they are stouter, wider and heavier, relying only on their sails for propulsion, but steered in the same way by a huge oar jutting out at the stern.

Tacitus tells us a strange story of how one night three of

Roman warship

Roman merchant ship

Agricola's warships were actually stolen. Apparently there was a cohort of rather tough German soldiers who had been put under a Roman centurion for training:

'They murdered their officers, boarded three warships and forced the pilots to do their will. Two of these incurred suspicion and were put to death; the third did as he was told. As no one knew anything about them they sailed along the coast like a ship in a fairy story. But the time soon came when they had to put into land for water and other necessaries. This brought them to blows with the Britons, who defended their property. Often successful they were sometimes beaten. Finally they were in such a plight that they first ate the weakest of their number and then drew lots as to whom they should eat next. In this fashion they sailed right round Britain, then lost their ships through bad seamanship, were taken for pirates and cut off first by the Suebi* and then by the Frisii*. Some of them were sold as slaves in Germany and passed from hand to hand till they reached the bank of the Rhine where they gained *notoriety* from the exciting account of their great adventure.'

So a few of these men actually managed to get back to their homeland—but as slaves!

In spite of this loss Agricola has made good use of his ships and in future campaigns they sail up the coast while his armies march on the mainland, sometimes camping together at forts which he has built by the rivers. Tacitus tells us that even in those days there was friendly rivalry between the army and the navy.

'The infantry, cavalry and sailors often meeting in the same camp would eat and make merry together. They would boast as sailors will, of their different exploits and

* Tribes living near the mouth of the River Rhine.

13

match the perilous depths of woods and mountains against the dangers of storms and tides, the victories on land against the conquest of ocean. The Britons for their part, as was learned from prisoners, were astounded by the appearance of the fleet. The mystery of the sea was *divulged* and their last refuge in defeat cut off.'

If we look at the map on page 5 we can see the camps or forts where soldiers and sailors must have met, Cramond on the Forth or Carpow on the Tay, where eventually Agricola built harbours and store depots for his armies. At this time too he is getting so keen on commando landings that he is seriously considering the invasion of Ireland, for he has given a feast for a refugee Irish prince, and thinks from all reports that he will have no great difficulty in conquering Ireland. However, his difficulties in North Britain are really only just beginning, as we shall see, and he will have a full-time job there for the next few years.

Another look at the map shows us a zig-zag line of forts running up diagonally from Bochastle near Callander. Now the ramparts of several of these forts are still standing so let us see what these Roman forts were like.

On the next page is a plan of the fort which Agricola's men built at Fendoch on the River Almond, guarding the entrance to the Sma' Glen. It is oblong in shape, surrounded by a high rampart of earth and wood. Outside this as an extra defence were two deep ditches, so you can imagine how difficult it would have been for the highlanders charging down the glen to make any impression on this fort, especially when, as they try to cross the ditches or climb the ramparts, the Roman soldiers will be hurling down spears and *missiles* from the top.

The fort has four gates, each protected by square towers on either side. They were made of timber with slit windows for the guards to inspect any visitors.

Let us watch for the moment as a messenger from the south

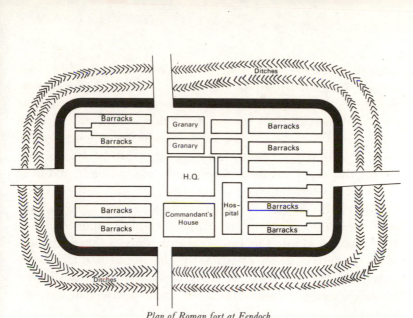

Plan of Roman fort at Fendoch

What the Roman fort at Fendoch may have looked like

canters up to the main gate of Fendoch, bringing the latest despatches from Rome for the governor, who is on a routine visit here just now. The sentry challenges him; he answers at once and then clatters in over the bridge and into the main street of the camp. On his right he passes the elegant front of the commandant's house, but ignores it for he knows that during the day Agricola and his legate will not be there but in the headquarters building next door.

Just as the fort is like Roman forts in every part of the empire, so the commandant's house is like Roman houses in Italy, Asia or Gaul. The only real difference is that it is made of local materials, not of bricks or marble as it might be in some other places. Like all Roman houses it has hardly any windows facing outside, but looks on to a courtyard on the

What the commandant's home at Fendoch must have looked like

inside called the *atrium*. This is perhaps a design of house more suited to the sunny climate of the Mediterranean than to North Britain, but it gives the commandant the benefit of privacy, and for a while at least he will be out of the sight of his men. If times are peaceful enough he might even be able to bring up his wife and family to stay with him there. But meanwhile the governor is present and urgent messages are arriving with regard to troop movements. Inside the headquarters building, which is large and square, there is a constant bustle of activity and there are little groups of men in the offices which surround the main court yard. Agricola thanks the messenger before sending him off for a well-earned meal and rest in the barracks.

We follow the messenger as he leaves the building and observe a wagon unloading corn beside the large *granaries*, for Fendoch is stocking up for the long winter ahead. He turns round, back past the hospital, outside which some wounded legionaries are resting in the sun. He gives them a friendly wave and passes on to a *barrack* block in the far corner of the fort where he knows he will find his old friend, a centurion of the third cohort. There he sits down to a welcome bowl of what we would call porridge and a cup of dark red wine. The men of the third cohort, who sleep in the long thin hut which stretches behind their centurion's room, are mostly resting or sitting on their verandas polishing their armour and repairing their clothes.

We can guess what the centurion will say to his friend when they have finished eating.

'You would like a bath, Sextus, I expect,' he says and the messenger smiles readily. 'I'll show you where the bath house is then, my friend. It's not quite as luxurious as the ones you're used to in York, I'm afraid, but up here so long as the water's hot, that's all we care about especially after a day's marching in this climate.'

17

So our messenger goes to the bath house which stands just outside the camp gate, and there he soaks himself for half an hour in the hot, steamy room. We shall look at a Roman bath house in more detail later on (page 63). Meanwhile the messenger has rejoined his friend and they settle down to a good yarn on the barrack veranda. Perhaps the conversation might turn now to the great new fortress which the legionaries are building further north, on the River Tay.

'It's big enough to house the whole XX Legion,' says Sextus, 'Do you know that they brought in six cartloads of nails alone, to help fix the wooden barracks and battlements together?'

Well, we know that this was quite true, because at the legionary fortress of Inchtuthil, near Dunkeld, on the Tay, were recently found ten tons of Roman nails. Some years after Sextus and his friend were talking the fort had to be abandoned, in a hurry. As the Romans did not wish the precious

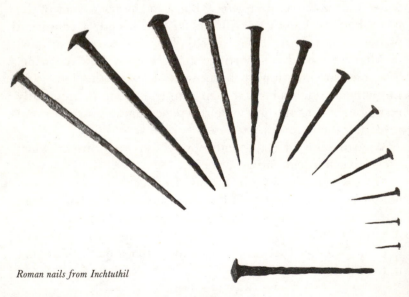

Roman nails from Inchtuthil

iron to fall into the hands of the enemy and be turned into swords or spears, they buried all the nails which had been used to hold the fort together. These were so carefully hidden that no one discovered them until a few years ago, and so tightly packed that only the top layer had rusted. When these nails were found they were sent to the laboratory of a famous steel company where they were analysed and counted. There were nearly three-quarters of a million of them, enough to send samples to all the museums in the world. Some of them were as long as 16 inches and we must remember that the Romans had to make every one of them by hand. Each one had to be heated up and hammered into shape from an iron bar till it reached the required length and shape. Then the head had to be made by hammering the thick end into a die. Imagine how many men and hours it would take to produce such a stock of nails. (Why could they be made so much quicker these days?)

But we are missing some of the conversation between Sextus and the centurion.

'Yes,' continues the messenger. 'The new fort will hold over 5,000 men, so you'll not need to worry so much; you won't be stuck out here on your own among these red-haired barbarians any more. And they're making some tremendous workshops, 200 feet long. They can make new wagons as well as repair old ones. In fact they'll be able to do almost anything up there from shoeing a horse to fitting out a warship.'

'But what's the idea of staying up here at all in this godforsaken wilderness?' asks the centurion.

'Well, Agricola says that if we don't stay up here and keep control of these northern barbarians, they'll keep on trying to invade the south. By Jove, there's not much to keep them up here, is there? Trees, mountains and bogs. That's about all there is.'

'Well in that case, let's just conquer the lot of them and get it over and done with.'

'I agree and so does the Governor. But one thing at a time. We can't charge through this type of country in the winter, knee deep in snow. We've got to take it slowly, specially the way these Caledonians melt into the woods whenever we want to fight them, then come back and ambush us when we're least expecting it. No, we've got to keep an eye on them, so we're building a fort at the mouth of each of their great valleys. That way we'll keep control of the bit we've got already.'

'But, Sextus, what worries me is that we're so far away from York. How on earth will they keep us supplied?'

'By sea,' replies the messenger. 'Agricola knows what he's doing. He's built this new harbour on the Tay, so most of our supplies will come up on ships instead of trundling all the way up that terrible road from the south.'

'Well I suppose we may see peace in this country yet, then', says the centurion. 'Come on, let's go and have a game of marbles with the other centurions. That's the only form of entertainment there is up here so far.'

Here we must leave the two friends to their game and see what happened during the months that followed.

3 The Missing Battlefields

Tacitus tells us that all does not go well for the Romans in the year 83.

'The natives of Caledonia turned to armed resistance on a grand scale. Without *provocation* they attacked one of our forts and inspired alarm by their challenging offensive. There were some Romans who argued that it would be more sensible to retreat back to the Forth, but at this point Agricola learnt that the enemy were about to attack in several columns. To avoid being surrounded by superior forces he divided his own army into three divisions and advanced.

soon as the enemy came to know of this move they suddenly changed their plans and massed for a night attack on the IX legion. That seemed to them the weakest point. Striking panic into the sleeping camp, they cut down the sentries and broke in.

'The fight was already raging when Agricola was warned by his scouts of the enemy's march. He followed close on their tracks, ordered the fastest of his cavalry and infantry to skirmish up to their rear and finally made the whole army join in the battle cry. Dawn was now breaking, and the gleam of the standards could clearly be seen. The Britons were dismayed at being caught between two fires, while the men of the IX Legion took heart again. They managed a sally and a grim struggle ensued in the narrow passage to the gates. At last the enemy broke under the rival efforts of two armies. Had not the marshes and woods covered the enemy's retreat, the victory would have ended the war.'

You will probably have noticed that there is one vital piece of information missing from this account. Tacitus never tells us which fort was attacked or where the battle took place. All we know is that there was a narrow passage to the gates, so it might have been Fendoch or Raedykes or any other of the forts. Perhaps one day someone will find some clue such as the burnt foundations of a fort or an inscription by the IX Legion which will tell us where it all happened. Still there are two important things which Tacitus does tell us: one is that for the first time the North Britons seem to be uniting in a single great army against the common foe; the other is that they are well led, nearly successful and certainly capable of giving the Romans a nasty fright. North Britain is not going to be such an easy conquest after all and the losses of the IX legion were there to prove it.

The result of the battle is *inconclusive*. The Romans were fired with self-confidence at their victory and determined to repeat it, but, as Tacitus tells us, the Britons were far from giving up.

'With unbroken spirit they persisted in arming their whole fighting force, putting their wives and children in places of safety and uniting in a league of tribes with a peace conference and sacrifices. They had realised at last that common action was needed to meet the common danger. Already more than 30,000 men made a gallant show, and still they came flocking to the colours—old and young. One of the many leaders was Calgacus, a man of outstanding valour and nobility.'

So here we meet for the first time the first known leader of the North Britons. He must have been a man of great strength and ability to succeed in uniting the tribes or clans of his country, and he seems to have been a fair match for Agricola as a general. Otherwise, unfortunately, we know very little about him. Tacitus tells us of a speech he made to his men.

'We, the last men on earth, the last of the free, have been shielded till today by our very *remoteness*. But today the boundary of Britain is exposed; beyond us lies no nation, nothing but waves and rocks, and the Romans, more deadly still: the brigands of the world who have exhausted the land by plundering, and now they ransack the sea. They create desolation and call it peace. Let us then, un-conquered as we are, ready to fight for freedom, prove what heroes Caledonia has been holding in reserve.'

So Calgacus pours scorn on the Romans.

Meanwhile Agricola has suffered his misfortunes. During the winter his only son has died, and he comes north again in the spring to try to forget his sadness in the heat of the battle. He too makes a speech to his troops and reminds them how often they have already defeated the Caledonians.

'These are the men who last year took advantage of night time to attack a single legion, only to be broken by your battle cry. These are the Britons with the longest legs—the only reason they have survived so long.'

So the two great armies come together—Calgacus with over 30,000 men, Agricola with not nearly so many, but all highly trained, well-disciplined troops. In the battle which follows he manages to fight most of the time without using his precious legions at all. He relies mostly on his 8,000 odd foreign auxi-liaries, mostly from Gaul and Germany, plus about the same number of cavalry from the same area.

Now we come to one of the strangest questions of all, a great historical mystery. Where did the great battle take place? Tacitus is a little more helpful than he was about the last year's battle, because this time he does at least tell us the name of the battlefield, Mons Graupius, or Grampian Mountain, but unfortunately nobody knows where that is. The nearest we can get is to say that it was outside one of the forts on the Fendoch–Raedykes line. All that we can hope is that someone will one day spot the vital clues which might tell us the exact place.

Meanwhile let Tacitus tell the tale of the battle.

'Calgacus placed his men on the hillside facing the Roman camp and the space between the armies was taken up by charioteers, clattering on in their wild career.

'Agricola saw that he was outnumbered and stretched out his line to the same length as that of the Britons. To improve his men's morale he sent away his horse and took up his position on foot in front of the standards.

'The fighting began with exchanges of missiles, and the Britons showed both courage and skill in parrying our shots with their great swords or catching them on their little shields, while they themselves rained volleys on us.'

What difference do you notice between this description of the British weapons and those of the Romans which we saw on page 7? The Romans have short swords and large shields whereas the Britons have large swords and small shields. This proves very important in deciding the outcome of the battle, for Agricola now orders six cohorts of his German infantry to close in and fight it out at the sword's point.

Model of Celtic chariot

Ancient wheel from Roman pit at Bar Hill. It may have been a Caledonian chariot wheel

'The Germans began to rain blow after blow, push with the *bosses* of their shields and stab at their enemies' faces— most awkward for the Britons with their small shields and unwieldy swords. Our men routed them on the plain and then pushed on uphill. This inspired the rest of our cohorts to drive in hard and butcher the enemy as they met him. Many Britons were left behind half-dead or unwounded, owing to the very speed of our victory. Our cavalry squadrons meanwhile had routed the war chariots and now plunged into the infantry battle. Their first onslaught was terrifying, but the solid ranks of the enemy and the rough ground brought them to a standstill.

'The battle now looked most unfavourable to us, with our infantry precariously perched on the slope and jostled by the flanks of the horses. And often a stray chariot, its horses panic-stricken without a driver, came plunging in on flank or front.'

The Britons now send in their reserves, but Agricola is ready for this and quickly defeats them with his cavalry. This is the turning point of the battle and many of the Britons try to escape, though some insist on fighting to the death. Others, when they reach the shelter of the woods take advantage of their local knowledge to ambush the first rash Roman pursuers. But as Tacitus puts it:

'Agricola was everywhere at once. He organised the combing of the woods round about and kept up the harrying of the broken enemy till nightfall. The British losses were 10,000 compared with only 360 on the Roman side.'

We must remember that these figures were given by a Roman historian and are perhaps a little biased. Anyway it was a complete victory for the Romans. Tacitus says:

'A grim silence reigned on every hand, the hills were deserted, only here and there was smoke seen rising from chimneys in the distance and our scouts found no one to encounter them. Everything pointed to an indiscriminate flight. Agricola took *hostages* and ordered his admiral to coast round Britain. When he took his army to winter quarters there was no tribe left which dared to oppose him.'

So ends Agricola's seventh year as governor of Britain and his fifth of campaigning in the northern part of the island.

It is now the year 85 and there is a new emperor in Rome, the unpopular Domitian, who thinks that Agricola is wasting valuable man-power on useless conquests, and perhaps resents the popularity which he is receiving from the common people of Rome after his victory at Mons Graupius. Anyway Agricola is suddenly recalled and is not allowed the usual triumphal procession through the streets of Rome which is the reward for a great victory. He is offered various new positions but advised not to accept them, unless he wants to incur the emperor's further displeasure. So, tactfully, Agricola retires from public life and keeps well out of the way of the jealous emperor on the outskirts of Rome. Perhaps even here he is not safe, for he dies a few years later, after a short illness; there are rumours that he has been poisoned, and people suspect the emperor's servants. Tacitus naturally has not a good word to say about Domitian who halted his ther-in-law's career, but even he

Coin of the Emperor Domitian

admits that there was never any proof of murder.

Meanwhile in North Britain the new governor orders Legion XX to dismantle their fortress at Inchtuthil and they do so in such a hurry that they have to leave behind their valuable supply of nails. The little signalling stations leading down the road to the south which would have warned of danger by smoke during the day or fire at night, are destroyed, and the other forts such as Fendoch and Ardoch abandoned. The Romans retreat to the line of the Forth and Clyde, perhaps even back to the Tyne and Solway—archaeologists are not quite certain when the forts between the Forth and Tyne were destroyed. At any rate most of what Agricola has struggled for in the north is lost, and the Caledonians are left free, severely battered, but able to recover from their heavy defeat at Mons Graupius.

4 Antoninus: The Second Invasion

More than fifty years have now passed since the great battle of
Mons Graupius and we meet a young Roman soldier pacing
steadily along a high rampart which stretches as far as the eye
can see. His name is Flavius Betto of Legion XX and he is
doing his daily spell of sentry duty on Hadrian's Wall. Every
now and then he glances up to the north to see if there is any
sign of movement on the rough moors beyond. Sometimes he
looks south as well, for there can be trouble in that direction
too.

Now you can see from the map on the next page that
Hadrian's Wall stretches from the river Solway in the west to

Hadrian's Wall today

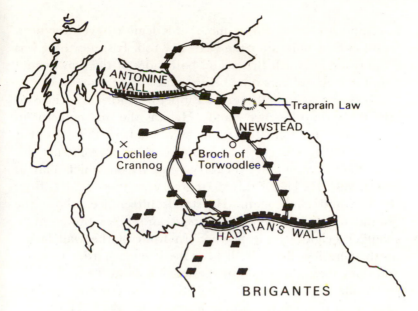

Map showing the two walls of Roman Britain.

the Tyne in the east. How does it come about that the Romans are expecting danger so very far south of where Agricola once led his victorious legions? Young Flavius Betto hardly knows the answer himself. His father had been a centurion in charge of building one section of this huge wall, nearly 80 *Roman miles* long and he had heard tales of great forts built in the northern mountains by Agricola. Some of these have been burned to the ground, others are now merely grass-covered ruins. Apparently the Romans kept garrisons in some of Agricola's forts such as Newsteads for about twenty years after he left, but eventually disaster overtook them all. In Flavius Betto's day people still talk in hushed tones of the dreadful calamity that occurred in those days when Legion IX was so terribly defeated by the North Britons that the Emperor declared it should exist no more. We know of this disgrace because no inscriptions bearing the name of this legion have ever been found in forts built after the year A.D. 100. It seems there was a big rising of North Britons on both sides of the Solway and many Roman soldiers died before peace was restored.

Lucky it was that the great Emperor Hadrian decided to take things into his own hands. He was the first emperor to visit Britain for himself. It was as a result of this visit that Flavius' father was given his job of helping to construct this great new frontier line, the very rampart on which Flavius now stands. He knows this stretch very well—500 paces from the fort and back again. He stands fifteen feet above the ground on the paved stone *parapet* and he is protected to shoulder height by the *palisade*. In front of the wall facing north there is a deep ditch to make it even harder to cross, and there is another ditch further back behind the wall on the south side to prevent ordinary Britons from crossing the frontier except through the proper gates. You have to be on your guard both ways—north and south.

Flavius has been stationed on the Wall now for nearly two years and in that time he has only once seen any fighting. That was when one of the tribes further north was causing some trouble and he was sent out with a cohort of auxiliaries to round up the troublemakers. Since then all has been quiet and Flavius finds it hard to believe that a whole legion could have been defeated in these barren hills.

Now let us imagine that we can join Flavius Betto on his beat along the wall.

'Hail' comes a shout and Flavius salutes Marcus who has the patrol back from the next *mile castle* to the point where Flavius stops. 'Have you heard the news? We've got another new governor.'

'Oh well, they come and go,' says Flavius. 'Who's this one?
Maybe he'll give us some action instead of just letting us wear out our boots on these paving stones.'

Hadrian

'You could be right,' says Marcus. 'It's the famous Lollius Urbicus. I happen to have heard a bit about him from a friend of mine who served in Germany.'

'Oh yes, he was one of old Hadrian's hard hitting generals over there, wasn't he?'

'That's right. He was on the Emperor's staff when he went to Palestine to put down the Jews. Then he was legate of a legion on the Danube and consul in Rome about six years ago. After that the new Emperor Antoninus made him governor of Lower Germany. He won the *Golden Crown* there—and now the Emperor's sent him here, so maybe something's going to happen at last.'

'About time too,' says Flavius with feeling. 'Tell me, Marcus, just between ourselves, what do you think of this Emperor, Antoninus Pius?'

Antoninus Pius

Marcus looks round quickly to see that no one is listening before he answers. 'It's hard to say, Flavius. I mean, Hadrian in his day used to come round all the provinces himself. You really felt he was interested, even in a god-forsaken outpost like this. It was his idea to build the rampart on which we're standing now, and a jolly good one at that, I think. It's made life a lot easier for the legions, because mostly we can leave it to auxiliaries to do the sentry duty. The trouble was old Hadrian worked so hard that he drove himself to an early grave, travelling day after day from one end of the Empire to the other. Now Antoninus is not the same type at all, though he was Hadrian's adopted son. He never even leaves Italy. They say he's happiest just staying at home on one of his farms. He's a fair man, not cruel like some of the rascals we've

32

had for Emperor, but he doesn't seem to have any great desire for glory or conquest.'

'In that case there won't be much for us to do,' says Flavius despondently.

'Don't you believe it. We'll be having trouble again from these barbarians. I reckon that's the news which made Antoninus send us this tough governor, Lollius Urbicus. The Emperor may stay in Italy, but I think he has a good idea of what's going on everywhere.'

'Well he must spend a lot of time making these new laws of his. Why, I hear he's even passed one to help slaves. Any master who treats his slaves badly or doesn't feed them may lose the slave. He's making things so that slaves will be treated almost like ordinary people; so no wonder they've given him the name Pius.' (= pious)

'Yes, he's very fair, but I don't think Hadrian meant him to be any more than a stop-gap Emperor. After all he was over fifty when he was given the empire, and he's never done any fighting with the army. I wonder whether he'll be strong enough if there's any real trouble?'

'I think so,' says Flavius. 'He is a good man and the governors of the provinces will want to do well by him.'

'Let's see then,' says Marcus. 'For there's trouble brewing up North and the Brigantes on the South of the Wall are getting restless again. They say Lollius Urbicus is actually on his way up from Eboracum [York].'

The truth of Marcus' words is proved a few days later when the new governor arrives at the main fort on the wall. For some days there are great comings and goings in the fort. News of tribal gatherings and preparations for war is coming in from all sides, and some of the fort commanders are worried about the safety of the wall.

One day Flavius hears a shout from his centurion calling the legionaries together for a meeting and we can guess what it was about.

'Right, soldiers,' says the centurion. 'We've been given our marching orders. Spring is here and the new governor himself is leading an expedition to teach these barbarians another lesson. They seem to be forgetting what the might of Rome is like, just because we have let them live in peace for a few years. We'll be away the whole summer, so you'd better say goodbye to your families, if you have them. We march in two days.'

So begins the second great Roman invasion of North Britain and we know very little about it. Unfortunately nobody wrote a life of Lollius Urbicus the way Tacitus wrote about Agricola. From the Roman history books comes only one sentence about this whole war. 'Antoninus subdued the Britons through Lollius Urbicus and after driving back the barbarians erected another wall made of turf.'

We shall be seeing more of the new wall in the next chapter, but so far as the war is concerned we have learned only that it ended in a victory for Lollius Urbicus. The best we can do is to try to find out a little bit more about the inhabitants of North Britain, the various tribes who have themselves left no account of these wars, because they could neither read nor write.

We saw that when Agricola went north he fought a people called the Caledonians and that under Calgacus the various tribes seemed to unite to fight the common enemy. These people were still living in what is called the Iron Age and spoke a language rather like the *Gaelic* which is spoken in parts of Scotland today. At this time they lived mostly in the Central Highlands and their name survives in the town of Dunkeld, which means Fort of the Caledonians, and the mountain Schiehallion, which means sacred mountain of the Caledonians. Later the Romans come to call this tribe and some others by the name of *Picts*, which perhaps means 'Painted People', but nobody is quite sure.

The Romans have handed down to us many other names of tribes who lived in North Britain, but it is very difficult to say where they lived or exactly what sort of people they were. The people just north of Hadrian's Wall, such as the Votadini, who lived between the Tyne and the Forth, seem to have been naturally more friendly with the Romans and tried to live at peace with them. This tribe was also *Celtic* in origin, but spoke a language more like Welsh than Gaelic.

However, though we know so very little about these people we do know quite a lot about the places where they lived and when we look into their homes we often find small Roman trinkets or coins or pottery which prove to us that these tribes must have come into contact with the legions of Lollius Urbicus.

There are four different kinds of North British dwelling places which the Romans must have seen and which we can sometimes still see today. First let us look at the strangest of all of these, the *broch*. This is a round tower about forty feet high and thirty feet wide. It is a cleverly built, small stone fort which is not found elsewhere in the world. We can see from the way in which passages run through the thickness of the walls and the spiral staircase leads to the upper stories that these North Britons are not so enormously far behind the Romans as engineers.

Most brochs, like the one in our picture, are found in the

Drawing of the broch of Mousa cut through the centre to show galleries and staircase in the thickness of the walls. Note the broch's entrance on the left

The Broch of Mousa as it is today

far north, and it is thought that they may have been built by refugees who sailed up there from areas such as Cornwall, when they were conquered by the Romans. However, we do find a number of brochs much further south in the parts which Lollius Urbicus invaded. Let us look, for instance, at the broch of Torwoodlee, near Galashiels. In it have been found some Roman coins, wine jars, glass bottles and other relics. Nearby stands the Roman fort at Newsteads which we saw was burned down some time after the death of Agricola. Putting two and two together, but still only guessing at the answer, we might say that some tribesmen destroyed the Roman fort, took away coins, glass and other valuables as plunder and then built themselves a broch in case the Romans came back to look for revenge. This the Romans would certaibly do, and we find that the broch of Torwoodlee was carefully demolished some years later. Perhaps at the orders of

Lollius Urbicus the broch-dwellers had to pull down their own home, stone by stone. The Romans would never allow such a strong little fort to survive inside their province and they were ruthless against their enemies.

Now let us turn to the second type of building which Flavius Betto and his friends must have seen. These are small hill forts, sometimes just a few farm houses of *wattle and daub* surrounded by a rough stone rampart and ditches. Some of these forts are larger and higher, such as the one we shall talk about in Chapter 10. Sometimes they are even the size of villages like the one on top of Traprain Law in East Lothian. This is the nearest thing to a town which the Romans find in north Britain, it is the capital of the Votadini and its strong stone walls enclose an area of 32 acres. Inside are many huts of wattle and daub, as well as some better buildings of timber nailed together with iron nails. These people are skilled crafts-men for whom the Romans have some respect. They have

Traprain Law, East Lothian, site of a great Celtic hill fort

many tools of bronze and iron and can cast beautiful metal objects from moulds. Many Roman coins and other objects have been found here to show that peaceful trade developed between the Romans and the Votadini. Even a Roman alphabet slab has been found, which maybe shows that some North British boy was learning to read and write the *Latin* language.

The North British have one ingenious way of making their stone ramparts even stronger. They place large pieces of timber inside the stones as they build and when the wall is finished set fire to the timber. On these hill tops they can create such a draught that the fire reaches an extremely high temperature and the stones begin to melt and join together. The result is an exceptionally strong rampart, and forts made in this way are called *vitrified* forts.

Now let us turn to the western side of North Britain where we find our third type of dwelling place. Flavius, who marched up by this route, must have been surprised to see what looked like small wooden islands in the middle of certain lakes. These are called *crannogs* or lake dwellings, so let us imagine that we can pay a visit with Flavius to the crannog found at Lochlee in Ayrshire. He has been sent with a comrade to inspect the crannog to make sure the people are friendly and not hiding any barbarian soldiers.

The owners of the crannog are obviously not expecting trouble as they have left a dug-out canoe tied up among the reeds. Flavius and his friend paddle over the lake and soon see that the mysterious island is made of wooden poles driven into the bottom of the lake. On top of this there is a platform of timber with a round thatched house in the centre.

Flavius steers the dug-out alongside a tiny jetty where a gangway leads up to the platform. Smoke is rising from a hole in the middle of the roof so they guess that someone is at home. They give a shout as they clamber onto the gangway and a long-haired, bearded man in a leather tunic appears at the

Drawing of the Crannog at Milton Loch, Kirkcudbright

door. He looks surprised to see them but shows no signs of reaching for any weapons or of running away.

'What is your name?' says Flavius in Latin, but the man shows no sign of understanding. He beckons them into the dark, smoky interior of the crannog. Flavius looks round carefully to see if there is any sign of spears or swords, but instead he sees a neat row of iron tools. There are pick-axes, knives, chisels, saws. A small pig is roasting on the fire and there is a large pot of barley nearby.

'These people know how to look after themselves,' says Flavius to his comrade. 'He must have grown that field of corn we saw beyond the lake and I expect those are his cattle grazing in the meadow. These are the sort of people we like to have in our province. We protect them from the barbarians so that they can till their fields in peace, and in return they pay the Roman army with a share of their produce.'

As if he understands what Flavius is saying, the crannog dweller at this moment pushes a steaming bowl of porridge in

Roman bronze brooch from Lochlee Crannog

front of each of the soldiers and they accept with a smile. This is how the friendship between the crannog people and the Romans grows up. In time they begin to trade with each other, as is shown by the pieces of Roman pottery, glass and ornaments found at Lochlee. There is another crannog at Hyndford, near Lanark, where over forty bits of Roman pottery have been found.

Now it is time to leave the crannogs and turn to the last and perhaps the strangest of the kinds of dwelling which the Romans see in North Britain. This is the *earth house* or underground house, a deep trench dug into the ground with stone walls and stone slabs for a roof. These are found mostly towards the east coast and must have been most dark, damp and unpleasant to stay in. Probably the owners in fact lived above ground most of the time, but in that case why have the underground part at all, since it was easy to attack and easy to find? Like many other features of North British life this is a mystery, but we do not need to give up because of that. We can all try to search the country for new clues about these ancient people and we can all use our imaginations to try to get a better picture of their lives. For the time being we are more concerned with their conquerors, the Romans who have now once more swept all before them as far as the line of the rivers Forth and Clyde.

Bronze saucepan with graduations from Dowalton Crannog, Wigton

5 The Building of Antonine's Wall

A year has passed since Lollius Urbicus first led his legions north beyond Hadrian's wall and once more we meet our friend Flavius Betto of Legion XX. He has done well in the past year and now he has been promoted to the rank of centurion to take charge of building a stretch of the new wall. Just as his father had helped to build Hadrian's great wall of stone, so now Flavius supervises this new one further north. It is made of turf and will later be called the Antonine Wall.

Now let us look for a moment at the map on page 29 which shows both the walls which the Romans built in Britain. What is the difference you notice between them? Their length. Hadrian's Wall at nearly eighty miles is more than twice the length of Antonine's. At each end of the northern wall the two great rivers Forth and Clyde form a natural barrier so that stone ramparts are unnecessary. Of course there are always boats to cross a river, so the Romans do at least have to build a few forts along the south coasts of the two estuaries, thus continuing the line of the wall.

The second great difference between the two walls which we can see from the map is the number of forts or black squares on the map beside each line. You can see that there are fewer forts on Hadrian's Wall, in spite of the fact that it was so much longer, so that these forts are much more widely spaced. Perhaps you can think of some reasons why the Antonine forts are so much closer together, and since no one is absolutely sure of the real ones, your answer may be as good as anybody's.

You may ask how it is that we are so sure that the bits of wall which we can see today between the Forth and Clyde are

In English the Latin name 'Antoninus' is commonly shortened to 'Antonine'.

Inscription from Balmuildy, Glasgow

the remains of the one built by Lollius Urbicus. In fact this has been proved by the discovery of *inscriptions* such as the one shown above, which was found at the farm of Balmuildy, four miles from Glasgow.

The tablet is broken, but even so you can pick out the letters LEG II (Legion II) and beneath that LOLLIO UR . . . The last four letters are missing, but this could only be Lollio Urbico. You will notice that the Romans use a V for their capital U. Finally the bottom line of the inscription reads LEG AUG, short for legate of the emperor.

Experts can often work out the meaning of inscriptions even more badly broken than this one and it is from fragments like these that much of our knowledge of the Romans in North Britain has come.

Now it is time to return to our new young centurion, Flavius and we find that his party of Legion XX has been given the western end of the wall to build, down to the banks of the River Clota or Clyde. This is one of the most dangerous areas to work in because attacks are always possible from the hills to the north. But they are well protected; a cohort of German cavalrymen keeps constant patrol and there are also some Syrian archers, strange men from the East, who are ready to pick off any intruders. It is one of the strange things

43

Roman arrowhead from Bar Hill

about the Roman army that it is the crack troops of the legions who have to do all the trench-digging and stone-laying, while the less well-paid auxiliaries do any scouting or fighting that has to be done while this is going on. To see Germans and Syrians protecting the frontier of Roman Britain reminds us of the size of the Roman Empire and the clever way in which the Romans used the conquered peoples of one new province to help conquer those of another. At this very time a new cohort of North Britons is being trained to fight for Rome in Germany—a great help there and a great help, too, to Lollius Urbicus as it keeps down the number of possible rebels in Britain itself.

Let us look at the structure of the rampart which Flavius and his men are building. First of all we see them dig a deep ditch on a line marked out by the legate of the legion. It is forty feet wide and twelve feet deep and most of the earth thrown up from it is put on the northern side to make the ditch still deeper from that side. Any Caledonian who wants to cross the frontier without permission will have a most unpleasant scramble under the eyes of the heavily armed Roman sentries, for the great ditch stretches with hardly a break for nearly forty miles. In one part of it, on Croy Hill, the legions have had to cut it through the solid rock, except for a distance of 80 paces where the hill is so steep that no ditch is needed anyway.

The ditch, however, is just part of the frontier. Behind it comes the rampart itself and we find Flavius watching the foundation stones being carefully laid by his men. This stone platform is fourteen feet wide and supports the remainder of the wall which is mainly of turf. We see the legionaries cutting squares of turf with their spades, carrying them up and laying

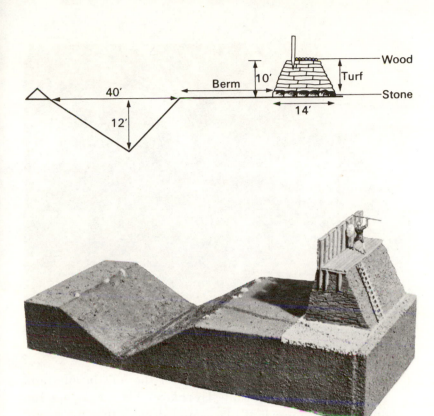

Model cross-section of the Antonine Wall. Note the stone foundation turf wall and wooden platform

them on the stone. The pattern of these layers of turf can still be seen today as black lines of *carbonised* grass in the brown earth, when archaeologists cut into the remnants of the wall to show a cross-section. So Flavius and his men struggle on and the rampart rises to a height of about ten feet. The turf wall slopes inwards at the top so that it does not become top-heavy. Part of Hadrian's Wall was also first built of turf and so are many fort ramparts, so Flavius and his men have plenty of experience in this type of building.

45

The Ditch of the Antonine Wall as it is today at Watling Lodge near Falkirk

The centurion casts a wary eye over the hills beyond and then turns back to his wall. He places his measuring rod against the side in several places and decides that the height will do. Then he details off a small squad of men to erect the palisade on top. Each legionary usually carries two wooden stakes for a palisade as part of his equipment, but these have long since been used up on the camps in which they sleep at night. Meanwhile they have been hacking away at the nearby forests; new stakes have been made and also timber flooring to lay along the top of the rampart as a walkway. All this is soon hammered into place and, as it is late, Flavius marches his men back to camp for their supper.

Back in camp one of Flavius' men, a Spaniard, who is a skilled stonemason as well as a good soldier asks him: 'Tell me, centurion, why is it, when our fathers built a very good wall for the Emperor Hadrian, we have to build another one here for Lollius Urbicus? What is there worth having for the Roman Empire in these hills?'

'I wonder that myself sometimes,' says Flavius. 'Certainly the Britons have given us some tough looking cohorts to look after the German frontier. But what do we gain from ruling the world? I suppose we almost make civilised men out of Spanish barbarians like you. And even my own country of Gaul was once a warring frontier place like this, in the days of Julius Caesar. Yet now we have *aqueducts*, *amphitheatres*, stone-built towns, roads, books and everything else the old Romans taught us. And here am I now a Roman myself, a citizen and a centurion in the army. And one day you'll be the same. By Jupiter even the last Emperor, Hadrian, was a Spaniard like you.'

'Yes, that was why he made such a good job of things,' says the Spaniard with a smile. 'So why this new wall? We're about ten marching days further into the wilderness and nothing gained.'

'Except peace, my friend,' replies Flavius. 'Lollius Urbicus is not so stupid. He sees he can divide these North Britons in half. The ones between the walls are mostly quite willing to live at peace with us, except for a few wild ones on the west coast. But if they join up with the Caledonians from north of here, then we have real trouble. This wall will stop that. Divide and rule, that's what old Julius Caesar used to say. Apart from that, we can hold all this new land without needing any extra troops, just because this wall is so much shorter. No, it's a cunning idea. Antoninus may never have left Italy, but he knows a good idea when he hears about it.'

'Well I tell you another thing that worries me,' says the Spaniard. 'Supposing a big band of Caledonians attacks a part of the rampart at a distance from one of the forts, how can one or two sentries stop them getting over?'

Map of the Antonine Wall

'They couldn't, you are quite right,' said Flavius. 'But if you'd spent as long as I have on Hadrian's wall you'd know the answer. We don't wait for them to attack the wall. The scouts let us know when an attack is likely—no army could get anywhere near the wall without being spotted the day before. This gives us plenty of time to have several fort garrisons called up to the danger spot. Then we go over the wall ourselves and attack them before they get near us. We go round the back of them and drive them southwards towards the wall so that they have no means of escape. That way there are few survivors. Anyway I tell you it will be years before the Caledonians pluck up courage to attack us again.'

'And what if they sail across the rivers beyond where the wall ends?'

'Well we're putting up some new forts down there already and also we'll have signalling posts all round the coast. So at the first sign of trouble the fires are lit, we see the danger signal and we send two or three cohorts down there at the double. That's what happens on the Clota side. The Bodotria [Forth] side is even easier, as we have a whole line of big forts there. No, as I see it, we have a very strong frontier here and I think it will last for years.'

We shall find out later just how true Flavius' words were to prove. In the meantime the legionaries settle down for the night as the Syrian archers continue their patrol.

It is not many months before Flavius' men put the finishing touches to the western end of the wall. As at the end of any great building the legionaries carve a special stone slab to finish off their work and on page 49 you see the one placed by Flavius on the banks of the *Clota,* by the fort of Old Kilpatrick.

Distance slab from the western end of the Antonine Wall

49

You can see it is in the shape of a small temple, and the goddess Victoria sits with one elbow resting on the globe (remember the Romans knew that the world was round long before the days of Columbus) and in her hand she holds a palm leaf. The great wreath in the centre of the tablet encloses the name of Legion XX, whose symbol, the wild boar, you can see carved beneath. In the top triangle are the full titles of the Emperor Antoninus and on either side of the boar you can see the distance of the stretch of wall which Flavius and his men have built.

PP.   IIII   CDXI
(Feet   4,411)

A tablet such as this is called a distance slab and a number of these have been found at various places along the wall. Today they can be seen in museums and help to tell us the story of the building of Antonine's Wall.

6   Life on the Frontier

We now come to the longest period of Roman settlement in North Britain. It lasts for about fifty years after the Antonine wall has been built. The same number of years in South Britain are enough to see big changes in the way of life of the native peoples. They had learned to wear togas, to talk Latin, to read, write and build towns. But in North Britain there is no sign that anything like this ever happened. Though we see the tribesmen of Traprain Law (page 37) using Roman coins, wearing Roman ornaments, trading with Roman merchants, even this is fairly unusual and the Romans never really seem to settle down to a peaceful existence with the North Britons. The different tribes like to acquire a few Roman luxuries such as jars of wine or glass bottles or fine pottery, but for the most part they continue to lead their own ways of life, growing corn, hunting, and preparing for the day when the first sign of Roman weakness will let them fight again for their freedom.

Roman life, then, along the Antonine frontier is not the same as that led by Romans in South Britain or Italy—a mainly peaceful life. There are no Roman towns or country houses, theatres or amphitheatres. It is a hard life, living always behind ramparts, always on guard.

However, the Romans are always good at making themselves comfortable, so let us look at the forts along the Antonine Wall and see how they fare. We find that our friend Flavius is now a garrison commander at a small fort now known as Rough Castle. This fort is the second smallest on the wall—only 200 feet square—and is the home of about three hundred auxiliary soldiers, Cohort VI of Nervii who come originally from Germany. Fort life is hard but it is a happy little community and Flavius is a strict but popular commander.

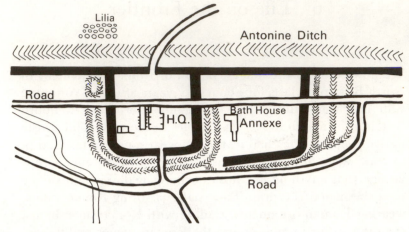

Plan of Roman fort at Rough Castle

The fort itself is very like a smaller version of the one we saw at Fendoch (page 15), except that its northern rampart is part of the Antonine Wall. There is a small headquarters building where Flavius lives and works. Alongside it stands the most important building of all, the granary, with its floor kept off the ground by strong stone buttresses. This holds a supply of food to last the cohort for many months. Outside the gates is a small bath house which the soldiers share with the tiny village of wives and children which has grown up on one side of the fort and is protected by its own special ditch. Quite a few of the Nervii have married North British girls and the number of wattle and daub huts in the village is growing every day. Flavius keeps a watchful eye on it, as he knows the ditch will be a poor defence if there is real trouble and this could as easily come from south of the frontier as north of it. He and his men must always be on watch, ready to send up the warning signals.

Flavius, when he first came to Rough Castle, noticed that there were the grass-covered remains of an older, even smaller fort and he has heard that the famous old general Agricola once had a fort on this very spot. Perhaps it was he who ordered the pits to be dug just beyond the north wall. These are rows of deep round pits *camouflaged* with bracken and with sharpened stakes protruding from the bottom. These make a nasty welcome for any enemies who try to attack from that direction. (They remind us of how this same idea will help King Robert the Bruce to win the battle of Bannockburn, not so many miles away from this fort, but more than a thousand years away in time.) The soldiers call these pits 'lilies' because they are the same shape as the flowers.

Today let us suppose that Flavius has been summoned to a meeting of garrison commanders at the wall headquarters, a fort about five miles away, so he decides to take the opportunity of inspecting the stretch of wall in between. He sets off eastwards at a brisk pace walking along the timber platform on the top of the wall. The palisade protects him to shoulder height and he smiles to think that only a year ago he and his

Rough Castle as it looks today. Note the double ditch below the archaeologist's hut in the centre.

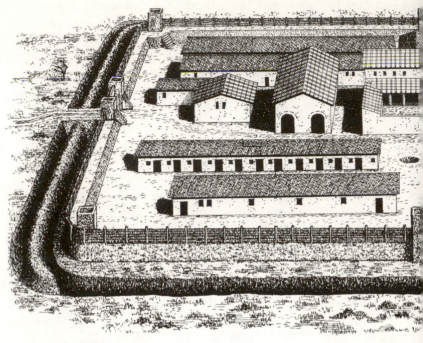

Reconstruction of Bar Hill as it may have been. This particular fort was set back from the Wall.

men had been working on the foundations of this wall which now seems part of the landscape. This section, he thinks, was built by Legion II. Not quite the same class of workmanship as Legion XX.

'Hail, centurion,' comes a shout and his thoughts are interrupted by the salute of one of his sentries marching back to the fort.

'Anything to report, Gallus?'

'Nothing much, centurion. Just a barbarian trying to drag a stolen pig back across the ditch. We'll be having pork for supper tonight.'

'Well done, Gallus.' And with these words Flavius continues

54

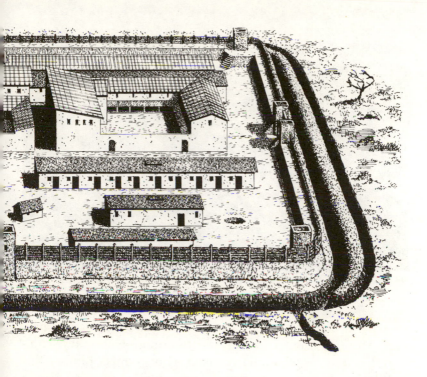

his walk. Shortly afterwards he passes one of the signal posts where a big heap of logs used for fire signals is covered with a leather tent to keep it dry. There is one man on duty, another sleeping below. Now Flavius begins to find it a little tiring walking along the wooden platform, so he takes the opportunity of using the steps at the signal post to climb down and walk along the road instead. This road stretches the whole length of the wall and beyond, keeping close behind it all the way. It passes through the centre of each fort but for through traffic there is always a by-pass to avoid congestion within the forts.

Flavius now makes quicker progress and is soon entering the fort next along the wall from his own, at Falkirk. He is saluted

The ditch of the Antonine Wall on Croy Hill today. Note the dip in the field below the trees on the right where the ditch has become less steep because of ploughing

smartly at the gates by the sentry and news of his arrival pro-cedes him to the headquarters' building, where the com-mander, a *prefect* of auxiliaries, comes out to meet him.

'Flavius, you must come and have a look at my new *ballista* before you leave.'

Flavius knows that the prefect is very keen on these great stone-throwing catapults and readily agrees to inspect the new one. This fort at Falkirk is quite large because it stands close to the only Roman road which leads through the wall northwards. About a mile north of it there is another fort at Camelon and then a series of forts leading up to the Tay to protect the tribes of this flat area from the Caledonians.

'I'm never sure how much use a ballista is in this country,' says Flavius. 'But I suppose it impresses the Caledonians to see them sitting on our ramparts.'

'Exactly Flavius. Anyway watch this demonstration.' They have now reached the northern gate of the fort, and there, standing on the broad turf platform beside the main wall, is the prefect's new pride and joy.

'They shipped it up to the Bodotria in parts,' he explains, 'brought it along the road in two wagons and we put it together here.'

'What's it shoot?'

'Stones more than half a foot wide,' and the prefect points to a heap of large round stones by the wall. 'Marcus, get the ballista ready to fire and we'll show the centurion what it can do.'

Two swarthy auxiliaries seize the handles of the ballista and start to wind down the great arm onto its horse-hair spring.

'See that tree over there?' the prefect says, pointing to a tree about 300 paces away. 'Fire when you are ready, Marcus.'

There is a loud twang and a crash as the wooden arm is flung upwards with the stone like a pea in a spoon at the end. A second or so later a branch of the tree hangs limp from the trunk.

'Good shooting, Marcus,' says Flavius, and turning to the

A Ballista

prefect, 'It's a pity it's not so easy to hit a Caledonian on the run. Still I suppose it might scare a troop of them. Anyway I think it's time we were off to the legate's for the meeting. I wonder what the news is today.'

Half an hour later they enter the biggest fort on the wall, now called Mumrills, a place capable of holding a thousand men, half of whom have horses as well, for this is the only cavalry post on the wall. The headquarters building is large and impressive too, with neat stone walls, smart pillars and a red-tiled roof. Flavius and the prefect march in past the pay office, the supply office and various other departments which look after the army's organisation throughout North Britain. Then they pass a sentry and enter the room of the legate in charge of the wall, one of the senior officers in Britain after the governor himself. The commanders of the three eastern forts are already standing there waiting for the legate to speak.

The legate is holding a letter which he has received from the governor. Like most Roman letters it has been scratched on a flat piece of wax protected by covers of wood. When the letter has been finished with, the wax can be scraped flat again and a new one written in its place.

'There is some serious news,' says the legate. 'There has been a certain amount of trouble near Hadrian's wall since

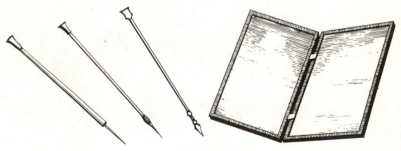

Writing tablet and stylus

58

most of the garrisons were taken away to come up here. The Brigantes are getting restless again and there have been several reports of Caledonian thieves crossing our wall, stealing food, sometimes even cattle, and getting back to their homes. This must not happen again. If there is any revolt by a tribe, it must not be allowed to spread, or the whole country will be in ferment. It is up to you to make sure your sentries miss absolutely nothing.'

After the meeting the legate takes Flavius aside and entrusts him with the task of passing on his words to the garrison commanders in the west, who have not been asked to attend as it was too far to come without leaving their forts for more than a day.

So the following morning we find Flavius on horseback riding westwards this time from his fort. He passes several heavily laden supply wagons on the way and by midday he has already visited the first three forts on his route. Soon he is climbing up to Croy Hill where he marvels again at the way in which the legionaries have chipped the frontier ditch out of the solid rock. Then on to Bar Hill, a happy thriving community where children play by the camp gates and the headquarters building has beautiful carved stone pillars. Here the commander asks him to admire

Altar from Auchendavy, near Kirkintilloch

59

Two more altars from Auchendavy

his new well which is over forty feet deep and lined with stone. A quick tug on the pulley rope brings up a bucket of clean, cool water.

Next stop is Auchendavy where Flavius stops for dinner and a chat with his old friend, also a centurion, Marcus Cocceius. This man shows him a new carved altar which he has just set up 'TO THE SPIRIT OF BRITAIN'. Marcus' altars can still be seen to this day, but we can only try to imagine how he would greet Flavius.

'You must think that I'm a superstitious fellow,' says Marcus, 'But I like to make sure that all the gods are on my side, even barbarian gods.'

Flavius laughs, for he knows that Marcus is forever throwing coins into wells, putting up altars and attending sacrifices. 'There are so many gods around these days,' he says, 'that I don't know how you manage to keep up with them. The Spirit of Britain. That's certainly a new one on me.'

'Well there's a spirit that looks after every country, isn't there, and since we live here we might as well have her on our side.'

'Fair enough,' says Flavius and follows Marcus as he goes into the inner hall of his headquarters to show the other altars.

'This is the biggest one,' explains Marcus. 'It is to Jupiter, naturally, the father of the gods, and to Victory also, for what can a soldier do without her help? The next one is to Mars; well we still have no other god of war, do we? But you see it is also to Minerva, the goddess of wisdom, to the Campestres, to Hercules, to Epona and Victory again. I put these in to please my auxiliaries here. They have all sorts of strange gods which they've brought with them from Germany. Now here's my own favourite, to Diana and

Roman stone carved pillar and capital from Bar Hill fort

61

Apollo, real Roman gods. One of these days I'm going to put one up to the Emperor Hadrian too, for he's a god now.'

'By Hercules, Marcus, the next thing you'll be putting an altar up to is that new Jewish god that keeps causing so much trouble. What do they call him? Christ.'

'No, no, Flavius. I'd only put up an altar to him if I were stationed in Palestine. But I'm in Britain, so her god it is.'

Flavius accepts this with a smile and is soon on his way once more. In the late afternoon he arrives at Balmuildy, a fine stone-built fort that guards the road bridge over the River Kelvin and stands in a commanding position facing the Campsie Hills. Then, after a few brief words to the officer in charge, he sets out again and five forts later reaches the western end of the wall. Little has changed since he was last there except that two merchant ships are tied up at the jetty beyond. This is the furthest up the river that ships can come, for it is wide but shallow and even at a lower point can be forded when the tide is out. This is why the two extra forts on the south shore of the estuary are so important.

The sun is now setting over the great rock beside the river (Dunbarton) and Flavius has delivered his message to the last of the garrison commanders, so he leads his horse to the stables and then turns to find himself a place to sleep for the night.

7　A Roman Bath

The following day on his return journey to Rough Castle the weather is warm and Flavius soon feels tired, hot and dirty. So it takes little persuasion for the fort commander at Cadder to induce him to spend the afternoon in his new suite of baths and to ride home in the cool of the evening. So let us take the opportunity of seeing what it must have been like to have a bath in Roman times.

The bath house here in Cadder is really no different from those in any of the other forts on the wall, but of course each commander likes to try his hand at special decorations or improvements in the heating.

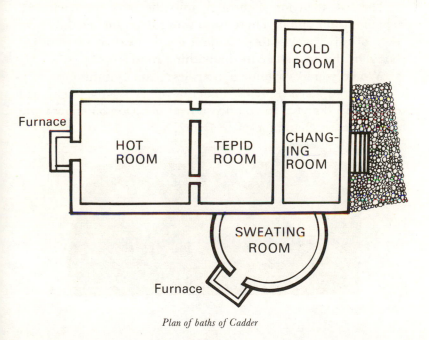

Plan of baths of Cadder

'We've had some trouble with smoke getting into our hot room,' says Flavius.

'Ours is perfect,' says the commander, a stout and genial officer called Quintus.

So they enter the small bath house from the cobbled yard where you can do exercises before going into your bath. Flavius, however, has had plenty of exercise and is quite content to go right away into the Dressing Room. There are two benches there and an altar to the goddess Fortuna, who looks after games of chance and therefore often has her altar in the Bath House, where marbles and other games are part of the fun.

'Take a pair of those thick sandals,' says Quintus as the two men take off their tunics. 'I promise you my floors are too hot to stand on without them. Now if you are ready come through to the Tepid Room.'

The two men move through into the next compartment, which is quite small. There is no water here, for the only purpose of this room is to provide a gentle heat to prepare the body for the next stage in the bathing routine.

'Would you like a game of marbles?' asks Quintus.

'Splendid,' says Flavius. 'There's an *as* in my purse next door and I'll give it to you if you beat me. Do you know I was once marbles champion of Legion XX?'

Roman marbles

Strigil

The next half hour passes quickly and Flavius proves that his skill at marbles is still as great as ever. After the game Quintus suggests that they go through to the hot room. Here it is very much warmer and they splash hot water over each other from a cauldron and a small bath at one end of the room.

Soon they begin to perspire freely in the steamy atmosphere and now starts the most important part of the Roman bathing routine. They do not wash with soap and water as we do but by perspiring and then scraping off the dirt with a curved, bluntish knife called a *strigil*.

While this is going on let us stop for a minute to think how the Romans managed to heat their baths so well. We know a lot about this since, as it was mostly what we would call under-floor heating, it has survived to this day buried beneath the surface of the ground.

The floors of the hot room are raised above the ground on pillars and the space between them is heated by a furnace or fireplace built into the side. So smoke and hot air circulate under the floor making it very warm. This is why Quintus had told Flavius to put on the special thick-soled sandals. Some-times some hot air also goes up through hollow tiles inside the walls, making the room even hotter, while the rest passes through a vent and under the floor of the tepid room which is naturally a little cooler since the heat is second-hand.

These rooms heated from below are called *hypocausts* and this form of heating is also used for the commander's house in some of the forts. Another clever idea which the Romans use

Remains of hypocausts uncovered at Balmuildy, near Glasgow

is something like what we today call storage heating. Large masses of masonry under the floor are heated up by a furnace and retain the heat long after the furnace has gone out. This means that a room can be kept warm over long periods without the furnace needing to be stoked very often. So we see that the Romans are real experts on central heating.

Meanwhile our two bathers have left the Hot Room and entered the cold. Flavius lets out a yell as Quintus flings a bucket of cold water over him and quickly takes his revenge. Then they sit dangling their feet in the cold-water trough before going back into the tepid room and then on to the Sweating Room which is as hot as the Hot Room, but dry. There are bottles of oil here to make scraping the dirt away a little easier, so they pour some on, pick up their strigils and set to work.

'Oh to be in some civilized place, where you have a slave to do this for you, eh Quintus?'

Hot room of Roman baths as it must have looked

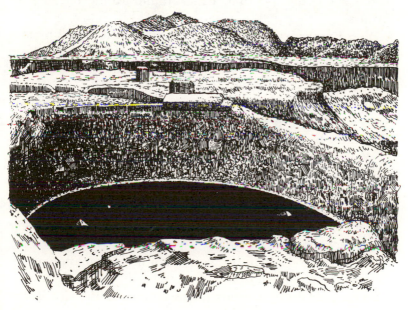

Cold bath at Mumrills

'Yes, who'd be on a frontier post like this? Why even in South Britain they have much bigger bath houses than this. But as for Rome I hear the latest baths there have room for thousands of people at a time and all the floors are covered with *mosaics*, in many wonderful colours. You could put this whole fort in the Hot Room.'

'Yes,' says Flavius, 'and what do the people in Rome do that they ever need a bath anyway? They go round and gossip to each other, then watch the gladiators or the chariot racing all afternoon, then eat and drink all evening. It's a wonder the Empire doesn't collapse.'

'I know, but I think Antoninus is not so fond of this extravagance. He's a sober enough fellow and he'd like to see the *gladiatorial* shows cut down a bit. The people have more of it than is good for them. Besides, for myself I'd rather do an honest soldiering job than hang around Rome begging for favours.'

'Yes, I agree with you,' says Flavius. 'But it would be nice just once to step out of here in our togas and see the palaces and temples and theatres, all in marble, or to see one of these really big shows at the *Colosseum*. Thousands of strange animals from Africa and the East. All sorts of gladiators. Or maybe a water combat with real warships battling it out in the arena. That must be a wonderful sight.'

'Well, Flavius, you may be a citizen of Rome, but I doubt if you'll ever go there. By the time you leave the army you'll be too old and tired to go all that way. Why it takes weeks even with horses and fast ships. No, you'll either stay here or perhaps go back to your native Gaul, but I don't think you'll ever see the seven hills of Rome.'

'By all the gods, Quintus, you've got no imagination at all. Pass me some more of that oil.'

So the pair finish scraping themselves, go to the Hot Room for a last hot shower, then back to the Cold Room for a quick plunge and a good rub down. Flavius is interested to see how Quintus has laid a new drain from the bath house. He learns how this goes into the main drain of the fort, helps to flush the latrines in the corner by the rampart and then carries all the sewage under Antonine's wall and well away from the fort. Drainage and the piping of water supplies is a subject like heating in which the Romans are real experts.

Meanwhile Flavius has put on his tunic again and taking leave of his host continues on his journey back to Rough Castle, feeling very much refreshed by his bath.

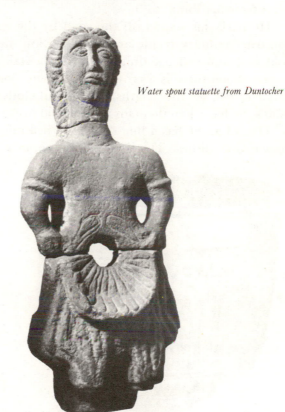

Water spout statuette from Duntocher

8 Salmanes the Merchant

The following day at Rough Castle occurs the monthly visit of Salmanes the merchant. He is a swarthy easterner who lives by the fort at the end of the wall, close to the port where much of his merchandise arrives by sea, sometimes from South Britain, sometimes direct from the Continent. His visits here are always popular, as they make a diversion from the usual routine at the fort and he usually brings gossip or news as well as interesting things to buy.

He parks his wagon off the road by the gates so as not to obstruct military traffic and there he and his fourteen-year-old son, also called Salmanes, set up a stall to display their wares. Soon there is a crowd round them, for the womenfolk are eager to see the lengths of beautiful cloth which he has to show. So let us join them for a while and inspect his wares.

First of all he has a fine display of beautiful reddish-brown bowls and dishes. This is the ever popular *Samian* pottery,

Red-glazed pot from Newstead. Note the eagle holding a dead hare. These pots were made in moulds, not on a wheel

which is the prized possession of many Roman families and is also much liked by some of the North Britons who can afford to barter for it, and prefer it to the somewhat cruder grey bowls made by their own potters. Some of these Samian bowls, which are mostly imported from Gaul have exquisite hunting scenes moulded round the outside.

Gates of Rough Castle as they might have looked

Left: Amphora (from Loudoun Hill)
Right: Bronze jug (from Lesmahagow)

For the most part Flavius' men use rough dishes made not far from the fort. They also have their mixing bowls or *mortaria* which mostly come up from the south; these have a specially roughened inside for grating vegetables. Then they have their cooking pots of black clay or copper, camp kettles and other kitchen equipment. Salmanes has a few of all these things for sale. Behind them in a wooden rack stand a row of large clay wine bottles called *amphorae*. Most of these have the maker's name or trademark scratched on the bottom and come from Gaul or Spain. As wine is part of the soldier's rations a lot of it is brought by army transport, but Salmanes usually finds that he is able to sell the odd extra jar.

Very many pieces of Roman pottery have been found in North Britain and can still be seen to this day. Experts can look at some of these pieces and tell you to within about twenty years the date when they were made. So you can see that when a new Roman fort is excavated pottery found in it may be a very important clue as to when the fort was built.

Flavius himself has now arrived at Salmanes' wagon and is looking for a new lamp.

'What do you want for this one, you old rascal?' he says holding up a neat little bronze hanging lamp.

'Only one *denarius*, Centurion,' says Salmanes. 'A real bargain and I'll give you a jar of oil that will keep it alight for seven whole evenings. Look, here I will fill it and light it for you.'

Salmanes pours some oil into the lamp and waits for it to soak up the wick which is sticking out of the spout. Then he strikes a flint and the wick flares up giving a soft yellow light.

'All right, I'll take it,' says Flavius. Then he admires some of the fine bluish-green glass bottles of different shapes. Some of the forts have their own glass bottle makers, but they cannot produce anything of this quality. There is also glass in the windows of the more important fort buildings.

Bronze lamp (from Loudoun Hill) (the chain is modern)

'What about some lovely fresh mussels?' says Salmanes (see what becomes of the shells—on page 76). 'I haven't many left and it's the last time I'll be bringing them, for by next month I'll have moved to my new house at the fort of Marcus Cocceius. We'll miss the shell-fish, but the new place will be more central for us.'

Flavius, like many Romans is very fond of shell-fish, so he buys a dish full of them and later he will take them back to his quarters to eat with his dinner. For this meal he will have a bowl of porridge followed by his mussels taken with soldiers' biscuits freshly baked in the oven by the fort wall. He washes this down with a cup of red wine. We notice that it is his favourite cup of Samian pottery and has his name scratched on the base. Not that he distrusts his auxiliaries, but you cannot be too careful with a Samian cup.

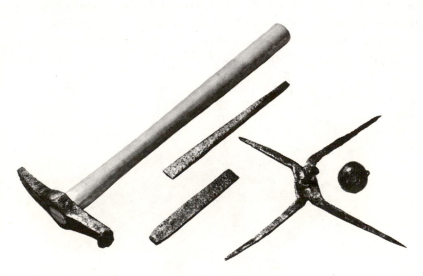

Roman hammer (the handle is modern), chisels, plumb weight (what do you think this would be used for?) and window cross for holding the four glass panels of the window in place (why do we not need these in modern times?)

Roman shoes from the well at Bar Hill

Next Flavius inspects some fine leather slippers. Of course most of the shoes in the fort are made by the garrison cobbler from North British leather, but it is pleasant to see more fashionable shoes from the south. We can still see a fine selection of Roman shoes because so many were found in the deep well at Bar Hill, thrown there perhaps by the Romans before they hurriedly left the fort. This well, in fact, has given us a lot of information about the Romans. Apart from shoes there have been found in it pillars and the carved stones called *capitals* which surmounted them in the headquarters building, ballista balls, bronze ornaments, iron tools and weapons, the pulley

Two brooches such as Flavius might have bought from Salmanes

and buckets belonging to the well, parts of a wooden barrel with its bung, some coins, animal bones and mussel shells. You can see why archaeologists today are always very keen to find the rubbish dump of a Roman fort.

After dinner Flavius remembers that he would like to send a present to the wife of Marcus Cocceius, who has entertained him on many occasions, so he returns to Salmanes who is now reloading his wagon and asks him for advice.

'Well, why not one of these pretty little British brooches or dress-pins. The ladies are very fond of them and I will hand it to Marcus himself this evening, telling him that you sent it.'

'That would be splendid,' says Flavius, and wastes no time in choosing an attractive little bronze brooch.

So we have tried to picture another incident in the life of our Roman centurion. We have had to use quite a lot of imagination, seeing the relics which archaelogists have found for us as they must once have fitted into the lives of their owners. When we look at the objects in our museums, it is fun to be able to do this—to see not just the brooch, but the person who wore it; not just the arrowhead, but the man who fought with it. Yet we must always try to find out everything that can be found out before we start to imagine the final touches to our picture.

Copper cooking pot (from Bar Hill)

9 What Happened to the Wall

We have seen a few of the happier moments enjoyed by the men of the Antonine wall, but soon a shadow starts to fall across their lives. We do not know what happened to Flavius Betto or Marcus Cocceius, we can only make a few guesses at the troubled story of the Wall. But the whole scheme of Roman North Britain seems doomed to failure. The Romans have been clever, but not quite clever enough. Perhaps they have taken on too much with an Empire that now stretches from the Clyde to the Euphrates, from the Danube to the Sahara Desert. With warring tribes looking for trouble on almost every side, even the Romans find it hard to cope.

No Roman history book tells us much about the troubles of the Antonine wall, but there are a few clues to the mystery. One is that many of the forts of the Wall seem to have been destroyed and rebuilt, more than once in some cases. This tells us that the North Britons may have captured and destroyed parts of the Wall once or perhaps twice before the Romans finally gave up the struggle to hold this frontier. Another link in this story is provided by an inscription found at Birrens in Dumfriesshire. This tells us that the fort there has been rebuilt by a new governor of Britain called Lucius Verus. Just before this many forts south of Hadrian's Wall have also been destroyed, and reinforcements for the legions have been sent direct from Germany. All this suggests a massive rebellion by the Brigantes as far south as York and we can be sure that if this happened the Caledonians would not fail to seize the chance of crossing the Antonine Wall from the north. This then is perhaps the first big break-through of the Antonine Wall, and must have occurred when it was not much more than ten years old.

Still the Romans are soon back again and Julius Verus seems to have quickly put the province to rights again. He realises that there have not been enough troops in North Britain, so he restores some of the garrisons to Hadrian's Wall which has been largely empty since the days of Lollius Urbicus. The fort on the main road north to the Antonine wall, at Newsteads is rebuilt to hold a much larger garrison, this time a *wing* of 1,000 cavalrymen, a mobile regiment which can quickly reach any trouble spot.

As a result of these improvements North Britain seems to enjoy its longest period of peace under the Romans—nearly thirty years. But after that again the Wall seems to have been pierced. We learn about this from the only lines in Roman history books which tell us about North Britain at this time. The historian, who writes in Greek, tells us:

> 'The tribes in Britain having crossed the wall wrought great havoc and slew a Roman general with the troops under his command. Commodus [the Emperor] therefore in great alarm sent Ulpius Marcellus against them. Ulpius Marcellus inflicted terrible punishment on the barbarians in Britain.'

We can guess that this writer is talking about the Antonine Wall, because there is no sign of damage on Hadrian's Wall at this time, whereas we have seen there are signs of a second disaster on Antonine's. This little story is completed for us by a coin issued in the year 184 which shows VICTORY in Britain, and that very year the emperor gives himself the title Britannicus to celebrate the victories

Victory in Britain

The Emperor Commodus

which his general has won for him in Britain.

Let us take a look at this new Emperor Commodus, adopted grandson of Antoninus, the last of this family of emperors. He becomes Emperor at the age of nineteen, when his father dies. He is a strange young man who likes to have his own way and hates the advice of the more experienced Roman senators and generals, who think he should accept their guidance. Instead he tries to make himself popular with the crowd by generous gifts and once even goes down himself into the *arena* of his amphitheatre to fight with a lion. Once established, he leaves the rule of the great empire to his servants and himself leads the life of a playboy. Many people die for plotting against him, more just because they are suspected. But in the end one of the plots succeeds and Commodus is found strangled in his bath. Rome is well rid of him and we can note that the great English historian Edward Gibbon, who wrote 'The Decline and Fall of the Roman Empire', starts the decline with the reign of Commodus.

Some people think that the story of the Antonine Wall was already over before the death of Commodus, for no coins have been found on it that come from a date after about A.D. 186. A more likely idea, however, is that it was in fact the murder of Commodus which led to the end of Roman North Britain. For after his death there is a *civil war* between three generals who each want to be the new Emperor, and one of these three is the governor of Britain, Clodius Albinus. To win his fight Albinus needs all the troops he can get hold of, so he takes with him the garrisons of the northern forts. While the legions of Rome fight with each other the Caledonians are left to swarm over the Wall. Almost every Roman fort north of York is damaged if not destroyed. The two great Walls suffer severely and Antonine's is never to be used again.

Meanwhile Albinus has emptied Britain of troops in vain, for he loses his battle for the Empire and kills himself in despair. The rest of the Roman world recovers slowly from the civil war but never again do we find the Romans trying to settle permanently in North Britain.

Gladiator fights two lions

10 Severus: The Last Roman Invasion

The man who beat Albinus in the fight for the Roman Empire is called Septimius Severus, and he is the only Roman Emperor who himself marched with his armies into North Britain. He is also the last Roman to invade North Britain and he does so, not to make a permanent conquest, but to teach the North Britons a lesson and to secure a peaceful life for the civilized people of South Britain.

It takes ten years to repair the damage done by the tribesmen after the departure of Albinus, to repair Hadrian's Wall and to rebuild the forts between it and York. By this time it is clear that only a very big expedition can hope to have any success against the tribes north of the Wall, so the year A.D. 208 sees the arrival of the Emperor himself together with his two sons. It takes them a whole year to prepare for the expedition and, thanks to the presence of such important people, the Roman historians have given us a fairly detailed account of it. One of them called Dio tells us:

'Among the still unconquered Britons the two main tribes are the Maeatae and the Caledonians, who have absorbed the names of the rest. The Maeatae live close to the wall which divides the island into two parts and the Caledonians beyond them. Their country is full of rugged and waterless mountains, barren and marshy plains. They have no walls or cities or farms, but live by grazing cattle, hunting wild beasts and certain fruits. Though they have plenty of good fish they do not eat them. They live in tents, have no clothes or shoes. They govern themselves and like to plunder. They fight from chariots and have small swift horses and their infantry are fast runners, very steady in the ranks. Their arms are a shield and a short spear with a brass knob on the butt so as to make a noise to strike fear into their enemies. They also have daggers. They can endure hunger and cold and all kinds of hardship, for they plunge into marshes and live there for many days with only their heads showing above the water. And in the woods they live on bark, roots and a certain food, a piece of which the size of a bean will keep them from having either hunger or thirst.'

You can make up your own minds how much of this account you believe. Dio had probably never been to Britain and so relied on travellers' tales for his description. Meanwhile Severus is on his way at last with a huge army. Dio continues the story.

'Severus attacked Caledonia and in making his way through it encountered unspeakable difficulties, cutting down forests, levelling hills, filling in marshes and bridging rivers.'

One of these bridges was perhaps the great *pontoon* bridge which he built over the Forth or the Tay, such as the one shown on the next page. There is very little trace of this expedition to be found on the ground today. Only at Cramond on the Forth, and Carpow on the Tay has Severus' army left behind many coins or other relics. We do not know of any inland forts or camps which Severus definitely used in his march northwards. So we must rely on Dio.

'He did not manage to fight a proper battle, nor did he ever see an army drawn up in battle formation. They drove forward sheep and cattle for the express purpose of luring the Romans to destruction. Our men suffered severely from the floods and when they got split up were ambushed. Those who were too badly wounded to walk were killed by their comrades so that they would not fall into the hands of the enemy. As many as 50,000 were killed.'

Legionary standard bearers cross a boat bridge

This last figure of enormous losses has to be taken with a pinch of salt, for the whole army could hardly have been as large, but the story is an exciting one and it is good for us to learn when to believe and when not to believe as we read accounts like this. Dio tells us that Severus reached the very far north of the island, but so far no trace has been found of his so

Severus

doing. Anyway at last the Caledonians are subdued. Severus issues new coins to celebrate his British victory and gives himself the title Britannicus.

But Severus proves to be a little early in his celebrations, for the following year the war breaks out again. This time it is the Maeatae who cause the trouble, and though attacked by the Romans they survive till the following year when the Caledonians decide to join them. Severus prepares to set out once more but his health is exhausted, and he dies at York, leaving his son finally to convince these northern tribes that it pays to live at peace with the Romans.

It is perhaps during one of these wars that a great siege occurs of the North British fort at Burnswark. This is a large hill-top fort high up above the Roman road through Dumfriesshire. We can imagine that some important tribal chief has made it the base for raids on the Roman province, so the Romans are determined to capture and destroy it. They build a Roman fort just beneath its ramparts and haul three great catapults up the hillside. These hurl huge stones up into the British fort, while the Roman *slingers* throw smaller missiles against the besieged. Lead sling stones dented by the shock of impact have been discovered on the hillside, so we can imagine that a tough battle took place. The Romans seem to have cut off the water supply of the British, for they begin a second fort, this time to the north of the Britons and surrounding the

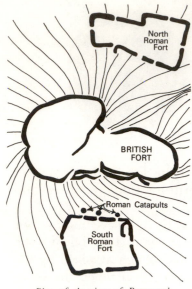

Plan of the siege of Burnswark

one remaining burn on the hill. Before this new fort is finished the Britons either burst their way out or surrendered, for the walls are not completed. Once the siege is over doubtless all three forts are dismantled to prevent anyone from occupying this hilltop for a while.

Before we leave this last invasion of North Britain we may pause to comment on its results. Wisely the Romans this time do not attempt to keep any land north of Hadrian's Wall for themselves. Instead they try to treat the people living there as their allies.

Two of the more peaceful tribes, the Votadini who live round Traprain Law and the Damnonii whose capital is at Dumbarton (the Fort of the British) come to be the special friends of Rome. Their little kingdoms stand between the more warlike Caledonians and Hadrian's Wall, so they act as what are called *buffer states*; by standing on the ground between two great enemies they prevent war.

This new idea of buffer states is most successful, for the peace that follows lasts for over a hundred years. Eventually the Maeatae and other tribes of the far north come to be known as the Picts, more dangerous than ever before, and soon to be joined in their attack on Roman Britain by new enemies such as the Scots of Ireland and the Saxons from Germany. As the years pass it becomes only a matter of time before the Romans leave Britain altogether, but in these final years the Damnonii and Votadini remain loyal to Rome and survive her fall.

86

11 Epilogue: Saint Ninian

We have seen that the Romans never succeeded in turning North Britain into a peaceful province of their Empire. The North Britons do not become civilized or Romanized like the South Britons. We may guess that there are two main reasons for this; one is that North Britain is such rough country and defended by so many hard-fighting tribesmen that it would need a very large Roman army to conquer and hold it down, at a time when the Romans have more vital tasks for their armies to tackle. The second reason is that Romans do not find North Britain worth the trouble anyway. We see that the efforts of Agricola and Lollius Urbicus do not bring lasting peace, but, if anything, seem to make matters worse. Severus, on the other hand, does not attempt a permanent conquest, yet succeeds in securing many years of peace.

The Romans do not leave behind any notable mark on the North Britons; their way of life changes little; they remain Iron Age people in spite of their contact with the much more advanced civilisation of Rome. The Votadini and Damnonii have not learned to build cities and bridges or write books or organise great armies. They have never accepted Roman rule for long enough to want to imitate them as the South Britons have done.

Mouldering ruins seem to be all that remains of Rome beyond Hadrian's Wall. But there is one small spark of light in the darkness. In the years just after the Romans finally leave Britain (about A.D. 410) a small white building appears on the shores of Galloway. The men who build it have been brought from Gaul by the son of a Pictish chief, Ninian. This man is a priest of the Christian Church which has been the official religion of the Roman Empire for its final eighty years.

Ninian has been to Rome to study and left it shortly before its capture by the Goths. Now with the whole world around him in turmoil he comes to convert the tribesmen of his native Galloway to Christianity. His tiny church is painted white and called the White House (the village is now called Whithorn).

The monks of the Middle Ages have handed down to us the story of how Ninian succeeded in converting the southern Picts to Christianity, but we do not know how long this lasted after his death. There is the legend that Saint Patrick was a Christian Pict from Dumbarton who was kidnapped by Irish pirates and then set about converting the Irish to Christianity. Certainly Ninian's pupils preserve Christianity in the North and West of the British Isles at a time when it disappears entirely in the South. Long after the Romans have left Britain the followers of Ninian are saying their prayers and reading the Bible in Latin and are carving in Latin on their tombstones. This is something which the Romans have left behind and which has been handed on through men like Columba and Mungo to modern Scotland.

DATE CHART

	IN BRITAIN	ELSEWHERE
B.C.		
55	Julius Caesar invades Britain	
44		Julius Caesar murdered in Rome
27		Augustus becomes first Emperor of Rome.
A.D.		
0		Birth of Christ
33		Crucifixion of Christ
40		Birth of Agricola
43	Roman invasion of Britain	
59	Rebellion of Boudicca	
69		Death of Nero
78	Agricola made governor of Britain	
84	Battle of Mons Graupius	
122	Building of Hadrian's Wall	
138	Lollius Urbicus governor of Britain	
142	Building of the Antonine Wall	
155	North Britons break through Wall	
184	North Britons break through Wall again	
197	Romans abandon the Antonine Wall	Civil War in Roman Empire
200	Hadrian's Wall rebuilt	
208	Severus' invasion of North Britain	
296	Picts attack Hadrian's Wall and are repelled	
310		Emperor becomes a Christian
367	Britain attacked by Picts, Scots and Saxons	
410	Romans leave Britain	Rome captured by Goths
432	Death of Saint Ninian	

LIST OF HISTORICAL CHARACTERS MENTIONED
(Emperors in Capital Letters)

Agricola, Gnaeus Julius. Governor of Britain from A.D. 78–85.

ALBINUS, Clodius. Governor of Britain up to 197, then tries to become Emperor but is defeated by Severus.

ANTONINUS (Antonine) Roman emperor.

Betto, Flavius. Centurion of Legion XX known to have been stationed at Rough Castle.

CAESAR, Julius. The first Roman general to invade Britain.

Calgacus, Leader of the Caledonians against Agricola.

CLAUDIUS, Roman emperor at the time of the conquest of South Britain.

Cocceius, Marcus. Roman centurion stationed at Auchendavy.

Columba, Irish missionary sent to convert the Picts in A.D. 563.

COMMODUS, Emperor during the last years of Antonine's Wall.

Dio, Roman historian.

DOMITIANUS, Emperor at the time of Agricola's invasion of North Britain.

HADRIAN, Emperor.

Marcellus, Ulpius. Governor of Britain in A.D. 184.

Ninian, Christian missionary in Galloway.

Patrick, Christian missionary in Ireland.

Salmanes, Eastern gentleman living at Auchendavy.

SEVERUS, Roman Emperor who invaded North Britain in A.D. 208.

Tacitus, Roman historian who wrote life of Agricola.

Urbicus, Lollius. Governor of Britain under Antoninus.

Verus, Lucius. Governor of Britain under Antoninus.

VESPASIAN, Roman Emperor who sent Agricola to Britain.

In the above list all are important and quite well-known figures except Flavius Betto, Marcus Cocceius and Salmanes. These three were just ordinary Romans, whose names have come down to us only because they were inscribed on stones which survived the years and are now preserved in museums. In this book we have tried to imagine what they were like, but we will probably never know if this is true.

THE ROMAN EMPIRE

In our study of the Romans in North Britain we have occasionally come across news from other parts of the Roman Empire. We must remember that Antonine's Wall is just a very short stretch of an enormous frontier, some of it protected by other walls, which runs right across Europe to the Black Sea, then down through Asia Minor to Egypt and back westwards across North Africa to the Atlantic. So the Roman Emperors have many other problems to cope with outside North Britain and while the Roman occupation of North Britain may to some extent seem a failure, the Romans elsewhere have a tremendous record for bringing peace and civilised behaviour. You can read more about this in the book in this series called 'Roman Britain'.

Map of Roman Empire

PLACES TO VISIT AND EXPLORE

If you would like to explore the remains of Antonine's Wall you should first read 'The Antonine Wall' by Anne S. Robertson, which is the Glasgow Archaeological Society Handbook. Your local Ordnance Survey map will also help.

Do not go to any Roman site in Scotland expecting to find too much. You will have to use your eyes, but once you begin to find traces of the ramparts it will be very exciting. Here are a few of the places worth visiting.

Roman forts

Duntocher—Golden Hill Park.
Rough Castle—near Bonnybridge.
Ardoch—22 miles south of Perth on Road A822.
Raedykes—near Stonehaven.
Burnswark—Dumfriesshire.

Sections of Antonine Wall

West of Watling Lodge near Falkirk.
Both sides of Rough Castle.
In Seabegs Wood near Bonnybridge.
On Croy Hill near Kilsyth.
In the cemetery at Hillfoot, Bearsden near Glasgow.

Museums and Art Galleries

Hunterian Museum, Glasgow University.
Glasgow Art Gallery.
National Museum of Antiquities, Edinburgh.
Museums at Kilmarnock, Kirkintilloch, Dumfries, Paisley, Aberdeen, Dundee.

THINGS TO DO AND MAKE

1. Explain what an archaeologist is looking for when he searches in the following ways: (*a*) takes aerial photographs, (*b*) tries to read inscriptions, (*c*) pieces together bits of pottery, (*d*) looks in refuse pits.
2. Imagine the class is the Roman Senate: make a speech defending Agricola and his work in Britain.
3. Find out all you can about the Roman army and make a book with pictures about it.
4. Compare the map on p.91 with a modern one and work out through what modern countries the frontier of the Roman Empire passes.
5. Write a play or a story about exciting times on the Antonine Wall.
6. Write a story about the life of a soldier's wife stationed at Rough Castle.
7. Make a model of (*a*) a Roman fort, (*b*) a cross-section of the Antonine Wall, (*c*) a crannog, (*d*) a ballista.
8. Draw or paint a Roman warship, a broch, a Roman centurion.
9. Paint an imaginary picture of one of the exciting battles or sieges in this book.
10. Make a toga out of an old sheet and a life-size Roman shield, helmet, sword and so on.

You can use the material from 7–10 to start a class museum, adding copies of inscriptions, coins, pottery etc. You may even be lucky enough to collect a few real Roman pieces—perhaps some of those nails.

LATIN WORD LIST

For classes doing Latin here are the Latin words for some of the
items mentioned in this book.

ala, ae, f. wing of cavalry
amphora, ae, f. clay jar
aquaeductus, us, m. aqueduct
arena, ae, f. arena
atrium, ii, n. hall of Roman house
auxilia, iorum, n. auxiliary troops
ballista, ae, f. military engine for
   hurling stones
balneae, arum, f. bath, bath-house
barbari, orum, m. barbarians
Bodotria, iae, f. Forth
Britannia, iae, f. Britain
Caledonia, iae, f. North Britain
castra, orum, n. camp
castrum, i, n. fort
catapulta, ae, f. catapult for
   hurling arrows
centuria, iae, f. century
centurio, onis, m. centurion
civis, is, m. citizen
Clota, ae, f. Clyde
cohors, tis, f. cohort
consul, is, m. consul
Corona Aurea, coronae aureae,
   f. Golden Crown awarded for
   bravery
currus, us, m. chariot
denarius, ii, m. Roman silver coin
eques, itis, m. cavalryman
exercitus, us, m. army
fossa, ae, f. ditch
gladius, ii, m. sword
hasta, ae, f. spear
horreum, i, n. granary
imperator, is, m. general
legatus, i, m. legate
legio, onis, f. legion
lilium, ii, n. pit with stakes

miles, itis, m. soldier
mortarium, ii, n. cooking dish
nauta, ae, m. sailor
navis longa, ae, f. warship
Picti, orum, m. Picts
pilum, i, n. spear
praefectus, i, m. prefect
provincia, iae, f. province
sagitta, ae, f. arrow
scutum, i, n. shield
senatus, us, m. senate
strigilis, is, f. scraper used
   in baths
stylus, i, m. writing tool
tabula, ae, f. wax writing tablet
toga, ae, f. garment of Roman
   citizen
vallum, i, n. rampart
villa, ae, f. country house

WORD GAME

For non-Latin *and* Latin classes.

1. Here are twenty words which the Romans used and which we still have as part of our own language today. See how many you already know. Those you do not know you will find in your English Dictionary. Some of them have changed meaning since Roman times.

consensus	tandem	versus	ulterior
quorum	peninsula	forum	posse
et cetera	rota	sponsor	minor
data	rostrum	conifer	major
maximum	via	interior	crux

2. How did our months July and August get their names? Your dictionary should help.

3. Many English words consist of two Latin words joined together. Look at these for instance.

   admit, permit, commit, submit, omit, emit

   You will see that they all end in -mit. Try replacing the -mit with -mission in each case and you will have some more words.

   Now see how many words like this you can think of ending in

   –vent or –vention
   –ject or –jection
   –serve or –servation
   –verse or –version

4. 'Castra', the Latin word for a camp has become -caster or -chester in many English town names. See how many you can think of. The word meaning a fort in the Celtic language was 'Dun'. See how many Scottish towns you can think of containing this word.

5. Mars, Venus, Saturn, Mercury, Neptune were all Roman gods. Can you find out with what aspect of life the Romans associated each of them? Then can you find out what they all have to do with the solar system. Here are some English words which all come from Roman gods: cereal, jovial, saturnine, mercurial, martial. Can you say what they mean?

95

GLOSSARY

amphitheatre, round or oval shaped building with seats rising up in banks all round its arena, used for fights between gladiators, and other shows

amphora, large clay wine jar with two handles, one on either side of the neck.

aqueduct, raised stone channel for carrying a water supply

archaeology, a study of past peoples based on the remains which they have left behind

arena, central part or stage of an amphitheatre

as, bronze coin about the size of a penny

atrium, large unroofed hall of a Roman house

auxiliary troops, soldiers in the Roman army who have been taken from newly conquered areas and sent to other parts of the empire to fight for Rome

ballista, large wooden catapult used for shooting heavy stones

barrack, long thin building in forts where the soldiers actually live

berm, ledge in between the top of a ditch and the bottom of a rampart

boss (of a shield), centre

broch, round stone tower built by the Celtic peoples of North Britain

buffer state, small state lying between two great enemies, thus making war less likely

buffeted, tossed about, beaten by the wind

camouflaged, covered with bracken and leaves so as to merge with the background and be harder to see

capital, carved stone between the top of a pillar and the roof

carbonized, vegetable matter which after a long time decays and becomes carbon, rather like coal

catapult, see *ballista*

centurion, officer in the Roman army commanding a *century*

century, company of eighty men; originally it had been a hundred

Celtic, belonging to the Celts, a race who came to Britain from Gaul before the Romans

civil war, war between two parties of the same countrymen.

Clota, River Clyde

cohort, six centuries make up one cohort in the Roman army

Colosseum, name of a famous amphitheatre in Rome

consul, title of the highest post in Rome under the emperor

crannog, house built on stilts or an artificial island in a lake

denarius, Roman silver coin

to divulge, to give away a secret

earth house, an underground shelter as built by North Britons, particularly on north east coast

Gaelic, language spoken by some of the Celtic peoples of North Britain

gilded, covered with a thin layer of gold

gladiators, men who fought each other in the arena of the amphi-theatres to provide amusement for the crowds

Golden Crown, awarded to successful Roman generals

granary, building for storing grain

hostage, member of a conquered tribe kept prisoner as a guarantee of the good conduct of the tribe.

hypocaust, system of heating by hot air circulating under a floor raised on small pillars

impunity, without being punished

inconclusive, without any definite result

inscription, lettering carved on stone

javelin, throwing spear

Latin, language spoken by the Romans

legate, officer commanding a legion

Legion, Roman equivalent of a regiment, consisting of ten cohorts, nearly five thousand men

mile castle, small fort on Hadrian's Wall

missile, any object shot by catapult or thrown by slinger

molested, interfered with, attacked

mortaria, special rough cooking bowls used by soldiers (singular—mortarium)

mosaic, floor made of many small, different coloured pieces of stone arranged to form a picture or pattern

notoriety, fame, usually of a not very welcome kind

palisade, protective wall on top of a rampart

parapet, top part of the rampart along which sentries walk

Picts, the name used by the Romans for the North British tribes from about the middle of the fourth century A.D. It is sometimes thought to mean 'Painted People', sometimes to refer to their fast boats called Pictae.

pontoon, boat moored alongside other boats so as to form the base of a floating bridge

prefect, officer in the Roman army in charge of a cohort of auxiliary or cavalry

province, the Roman Empire was divided into provinces, each under a *governor*

provocation, giving cause for someone else to make war

rampart, thick wall of earth or stone used to defend forts or frontiers

reconnoitring, scouts going over an area to see how the land lies before an attack is made

remoteness, being far away

Roman mile, about 1,620 English yards

Samian ware, special type of reddish-brown pottery mostly imported to Roman Britain from Gaul

senate, great council at Rome, roughly equivalent to our House of Lords

slingers, auxiliary soldiers whose main weapon was a sling for throwing stones or lead pellets

standard, decorated pole with various sacred symbols attached to it, each legion had its own, carried into battle by a standard-bearer

strigil, curved, blunt knife used for scraping dirt and perspiration off your body in a Roman bath

toga, special garment worn by Roman citizens: a single long piece of cloth (about 18 feet by 7 feet) with one straight edge and one curved. This was draped round the body in different ways

vitrified, turned to glass, melted by fire and hardened again

wattle and daub, wall built of reeds or sticks woven into a timber framework and then covered with mud or clay

wing, regiment of cavalry, about 600 or 1,000 men